Phishing, Vishing, & Smishing…Oh My!

How to Outsmart Digital Con Artists Before They Multiply Like Rabbits

MARC WEATHERS

Copyright © 2025 Red Rabbit Publishing

All rights reserved.

All rights reserved. No part of this publication may be reproduced, distributed, or transmitted in any form or by any means, including photocopying, recording, or other electronic or mechanical methods, or by any information storage and retrieval system without prior written permission of the publisher, except in the case of very brief quotations embodied in critical reviews and certain other noncommercial uses permitted by copyright law.

This book is designed to provide accurate and authoritative information regarding the subject matter herein. It is sold with the understanding that the author and publisher are not engaged in rendering legal, accounting, or other professional services. If you require legal advice or other expert assistance, you should seek the services of a competent professional.

While the author has made every effort to provide accurate website addresses and other information at the time of publication, neither the publisher nor the author assumes any responsibility for errors or changes that occur after publication. Further, the publisher does not have any control over and does not assume any responsibility for author or third-party websites or their content.

1st Edition 2025

ISBN: 979-8-218-70805-4

Dedication

This book is dedicated to the countless individuals worldwide who have fallen victim to phishing, smishing, and vishing scams. Your experiences, often untold and deeply personal, underscore the critical need for accessible, actionable information on cybersecurity. This work stands as a testament to your resilience and a call for greater awareness and proactive protection against these insidious threats. It is a tribute to your strength in the face of adversity, a reminder that no one is immune, and a hope that this guide empowers you - and others - to navigate the digital landscape with greater confidence and security.

This book is also dedicated to the unsung heroes of cybersecurity – the researchers, analysts, and security professionals who work relentlessly to expose criminal activities, develop innovative defenses, and educate the public. Your efforts to protect individuals and organizations from online threats are invaluable, and your dedication inspires us to continually refine our understanding and response to the ever-evolving landscape of cybercrime. We stand in admiration of your expertise and unwavering commitment to digital safety.

Moreover, this dedication extends to the families and friends who support victims of these attacks, offering solace, guidance, and steadfast belief. The emotional toll of cybercrime reaches far beyond the individual, affecting loved ones and communities. Your compassion and support are vital in the healing process and in fostering a society that prioritizes digital wellbeing. Your contribution to the collective effort to combat cybercrime is immeasurable.

Finally, this book is dedicated to the future generation of digital citizens. We hope this guide serves as a valuable resource for young people navigating an increasingly complex and interconnected digital world. By understanding the threats of phishing, smishing, and vishing, you can equip yourselves with the knowledge and skills to protect both yourselves and your communities from the perils of online fraud. Your safety and security are paramount, and this book is a testament to the importance of empowering the next generation to be confident and safe online. We believe in your ability to create a safer, more secure digital future for all.

Contents

INTRODUCTION: The Rise of Phishing, Smishing, and Vishing — 1

Chapter 1: Identifying the Red Flags of Suspicious Communication — 7

Chapter 2: Technical Mechanisms of Phishing Attacks — 13

Chapter 3: Analyzing the Psychology of Social Engineering — 19

Chapter 4: Case Studies – Real World Examples of Phishing Attacks — 25

Chapter 5: Email Security Best Practices — 31

Chapter 6: Securing Your Mobile Devices — 37

Chapter 7: Password Management Strategies — 43

Chapter 8: Safe Online Behavior and Practices — 47

Chapter 9: Recognizing and Reporting Suspicious Websites — 53

Chapter 10: Identifying Vishing Calls – Red Flags and Warning Signs — 59

Chapter 11: Techniques for Handling Suspicious Calls — 65

Chapter 12: Protecting Your Phone and Voicemail	71
Chapter 13: Call Authentication and Verification Methods	77
Chapter 14: Understanding Smishing Tactics and Techniques	87
Chapter 15: Identifying Malicious SMS Messages	93
Chapter 16: Mobile Security Best Practices for Smishing Prevention	99
Chapter 17: Responding to Suspicious SMS Messages	105
Chapter 18: Case Studies – Real World Smishing Scams	111
Chapter 19: Spear Phishing and Whaling Attacks	117
Chapter 20: The Role of Malware in Phishing Attacks	123
Chapter 21: Phishing Kits and Attack Infrastructure	129
Chapter 22: Detecting and Preventing Advanced Phishing Attacks	135
Chapter 23: Case Studies – Advanced Phishing Campaigns	141
Chapter 24: Immediate Actions After a Suspected Phishing Attack	147
Chapter 25: Reporting Phishing Attempts to Authorities	153
Chapter 26: Mitigating Potential Damage	159
Chapter 27: Legal and Financial Recourse	165
Chapter 28: Rebuilding Trust and Preventing Future Attacks	171
Acknowledgements	177

Appendix	179
Glossary	191
References	193
ABOUT THE AUTHOR	195

INTRODUCTION: The Rise of Phishing, Smishing, and Vishing

The insidious nature of phishing, smishing, and vishing attacks has evolved dramatically over the past two decades, transforming from relatively crude attempts at deception to highly sophisticated, targeted campaigns capable of inflicting significant financial and reputational damage. Understanding this evolution is crucial to effectively combating these threats. Early phishing attacks primarily relied on simple email messages containing malicious links or attachments, often targeting unsuspecting users with generic promises or threats. These initial attempts, while often clumsy in execution, proved remarkably effective due to a general lack of awareness about online security best practices among the average internet user.

The motivations of cybercriminals behind these attacks are primarily financial. The theft of personal and financial information - including credit card details, bank account numbers, and social security numbers - remains the primary objective. This stolen data can be sold on the dark web, used for identity theft, or leveraged for further fraudulent activity. However, the motivations often extend beyond monetary gain. In some instances, attackers aim to disrupt critical infrastructure or spread malware, causing widespread damage and chaos. State-sponsored actors may also employ these tactics for espionage or sabotage, targeting specific individuals or organizations to access sensitive information or hinder operations.

The evolution of attack vectors has mirrored advancements in technology. What began with a reliance on email has expanded to include text messages (smishing) and phone calls (vishing), exploiting the ubiquity of mobile devices and the inherent trust often placed in phone communications - especially those appearing to come from legitimate organizations. Attackers constantly adapt their techniques, using increasingly sophisticated social engineering tactics to manipulate victims and bypass security measures. This includes crafting highly personalized messages, exploiting current events or trending topics to enhance credibility, and leveraging urgency or fear to pressure victims into immediate action.

The consequences of successful phishing, smishing, and vishing attacks can be far-reaching and devastating. Financial losses may range from relatively minor amounts to significant sums, depending on the target and the sophistication of the attack. Reputational damage can be just as severe, particularly for organizations hit by high-profile breaches. The loss of customer trust, harm to brand image, and potential legal repercussions can all threaten an organization's long-term viability. Additionally, successful attacks can expose sensitive personal information, leading to identity theft, fraud, and other serious consequences for individuals. This includes compromised medical records, legal documents, and personal financial information - all of which can be exploited for malicious purposes.

Several high-profile examples illustrate the devastating impact of these attacks. The 2024 Change Healthcare Phishing breach, for example, compromised 100 million user accounts, exposing personal health information such as health records, social security numbers, passwords, email addresses, and security questions. The incident resulted in significant financial losses, reputational damage for the company, and emotional distress for affected users. Similarly, the 2024 Pepco Group business email compromise Cybercriminals targeted the company's Hungarian branch with emails crafted using advanced AI tools to mimic internal communications. These deceptive messages facilitated fraudulent money transfers, resulting in a financial loss of approximately €15.5 million. - highlighting the vulnerabilities within even seemingly secure systems. These incidents underscored the critical need for strong security measures and heightened awareness of phishing threats across all sectors.

The current threat landscape is marked by the relentless evolution of attack techniques. Cybercriminals are constantly devising new and innovative methods to bypass security measures and exploit human vulnerabilities. The rise of artificial intelligence (AI) in phishing attacks has enabled the automated creation of highly personalized and convincing messages, allowing attackers to scale their efforts and making detection and prevention increasingly difficult. This dynamic environment demands a proactive, adaptable approach to cybersecurity - requiring both individuals and organizations to remain vigilant and continually update their security protocols to stay ahead of emerging threats.

Combating these sophisticated attacks presents significant challenges. The sheer volume of phishing attempts makes it difficult for security systems to detect and block every malicious communication. The constant evolution of attack techniques also renders many traditional security measures ineffective. Human vulnerabilities remain a critical weak point, as attackers continue to exploit trust and emotional manipulation to bypass even the most robust technological safeguards. A multifaceted approach - combining advanced technological solutions, strong security protocols, and comprehensive user education - is essential to effectively address the growing threat posed by phishing, smishing, and vishing attacks.

The sheer scale of the problem necessitates a concerted effort from multiple stakeholders. Governments must play a crucial role in developing and enforcing regulations to protect consumers and businesses. Technology companies need to invest in innovative security solutions and equip users with clear, effective tools to defend themselves.

Finally, individuals and organizations must take responsibility for their own digital security by investing time and resources in education and adopting proactive security measures. Only through a collaborative approach can we effectively confront the ever-evolving threat landscape and mitigate the substantial risks posed by phishing, smishing, and vishing attacks.

The financial impact of successful attacks is substantial and often underestimated.

Beyond direct losses, there are significant indirect costs tied to incident response, legal fees, reputational repair, and business disruption. Companies targeted by these attacks frequently incur expenses for forensic investigations, remediation of compromised systems, and notification of affected customers. Reputational damage can lead to lost business, diminished customer loyalty, and reduced investor confidence. This highlights the critical importance of preventative measures and robust incident response plans to minimize the financial fallout of a successful attack.

The psychological impact on victims is also significant, often resulting in feelings of frustration, anger, embarrassment, and even depression. The violation of personal privacy and the loss of financial resources can cause substantial emotional distress. Victims may lose trust in online services and institutions, leading to reduced engagement in digital activities. The emotional toll should not be underestimated, and supportive resources - including counseling - should be readily available to assist those affected by these attacks.

The legal ramifications of phishing, smishing, and vishing attacks can be substantial. Companies that fail to adequately protect customer data may face law suits and regulatory penalties. Individuals who fall victim to identity theft may also seek legal remedies to recover financial losses and repair reputational damage. As the legal landscape surrounding these attacks continues to evolve, it is essential for both individuals and organizations to stay informed about their rights and responsibilities.

In conclusion, the rise of phishing, smishing, and vishing attacks poses a significant and continually evolving threat to individuals and organizations. The motivations of cybercriminals, the growing sophistication of attack vectors, and the wide-ranging consequences of successful breaches demand a proactive, multifaceted approach to mitigation. This requires a commitment to ongoing education, robust security measures, and collaboration among governments, technology companies, and users to effectively combat these pervasive threats. The information presented here is intended to empower readers with a deeper understanding of these attacks, equipping them to take the necessary preventative steps to protect themselves and their organizations.

Chapter 1: Identifying the Red Flags of Suspicious Communication

The preceding chapters have established the pervasive nature of phishing, smishing, and vishing attacks, highlighting their evolution and the serious consequences for both individuals and organizations. Now, let's dive into the practical side: identifying these deceptive communications. Recognizing the red flags is your first line of defense, empowering you to stay one step ahead and avoid becoming a victim.

One of the most crucial aspects of identifying suspicious communication is recognizing the subtle cues attackers use to mask their malicious intent. These attacks often rely on social engineering, exploiting human psychology by playing on trust and urgency. Rather than blatantly demanding your information, attackers craft messages that appear legitimate and trustworthy, often mimicking the style and tone of genuine organizations.

Email Phishing Attacks

Let's start with email phishing. A seemingly innocuous email - maybe from your bank or well-known online retailer - might contain several subtle but telling red flags.

First, scrutinize the sender's email address. While sophisticated attackers can create very similar-looking addresses, a closer look often reveals minor discrepancies—a slightly misspelled domain, an extra character, or an unusual top-level domain (TLD). For example, a fraudulent email might come from "paypal.com.co" instead of the legitimate "paypal.com," a subtle difference that's easy to miss when you're rushing. Pay close attention to this detail; it's often the first sign of a potential scam.

The language used in the email is another crucial indicator. Legitimate organizations typically use professional, grammatically correct language. Phishing emails, on the other hand, often contain poor grammar, spelling errors, and awkward phrasing. These inconsistencies are telltale signs of a hastily constructed message, revealing the sender's true intentions. Also, be cautious of emails that swing too far either way - too formal or too casual. For example, a genuine message from a bank would rarely use overly casual language.

Urgency is another common tactic phishers use. They create a sense of immediate action, urging you to respond quickly to avoid penalties or miss out on opportunities. Phrases like *"Your account has been compromised," "Urgent action required,"* or *"Limited-time offer"* are designed to trigger fear or excitement, prompting rash, immediate responses. Legitimate organizations rarely communicate with this kind of urgency. Take your time – there's almost never a genuine reason to act immediately.

Suspicious links and attachments are among the most obvious red flags in phishing emails. Hover your mouse over any link before clicking to reveal the actual URL. This simple step can show whether the link redirects to a legitimate website or a malicious one. Similarly, avoid opening attachments from unknown senders or those you weren't unexpecting. These attachments may contain malware designed to infect your computer and steal personal information. If you're ever unsure about an email's authenticity, it's safer to err on the side of caution and contact the purported sender directly through a verified channel - like the organization's official website - to confirm the communication.

Text Message Smishing Attacks

Now, let's turn our attention to smishing attacks, which use text messages to deceive victims. The red flags are much like those in email phishing.

First, examine the sender's phone number. Be cautious of unfamiliar numbers or those that don't match the organization the message claims to represent. Next, scrutinize the message itself for poor grammar, spelling mistakes, or unusual phrasing. Like email phishing, smishing often relies on urgent requests, demanding immediate action or threatening severe consequences if you don't respond. Shortened URLs - which hide the true destination - are common in smishing attacks, masking malicious websites. Never click links in unsolicited text messages; always verify the sender's identity through a trusted, independent channel before taking any action.

Voice Mail Vishing Attacks

Vishing, or voice phishing, presents a slightly different set of red flags, though the underlying principles remain the same. Be wary of unsolicited calls, especially those requesting personal information. Legitimate organizations rarely ask for sensitive details over the phone. Pay attention to the caller's tone and demeanor - if they sound overly aggressive, insistent, or unfamiliar with your account details, be suspicious. A sophisticated vishing attack might involve a spoofed caller ID to appear as a legitimate organization; however, genuine organizations typically offer several verifiable contact methods beyond a single phone number. Never provide personal information to an unsolicited caller, and always verify their identity through an independent, legitimate channel before disclosing any sensitive details.

Real-world examples further illustrate these red flags.

Imagine receiving an email that appears to be from your bank, informing you of a suspicious login attempt and asking you to verify your account details by clicking a link. While the email might look convincingly authentic, the sender's address could contain a minor spelling error or an unusual TLD – top-level domain. Or perhaps the message uses strangely formal or informal language compared to your bank's usual communication style. These subtle differences are telltale signs of a phishing attack.

Another example might involve a text message claiming to be from a courier service, requesting a small fee to receive a package. The message could include a shortened URL or ask for personal information – both signs of a smishing attempt.

Finally, consider an unsolicited call from someone claiming to be from the IRS, threatening legal action unless you immediately pay a tax debt. The caller's aggressive tone, coupled with the request for sensitive financial information, clearly indicates a vishing attempt.

To reinforce these learnings, consider the following checklist:

- **Examine the sender's address or phone number:** Does it match the expected organization?

- **Assess the language used:** Is it grammatically correct and professionally written?

- **Look for urgency:** Does the communication try to create a sense of pressure or fear?

- **Check links and attachments:** Are they legitimate?

- **Verify the communication:** Contact the purported sender directly through a trusted, independent channel.

By diligently applying this checklist to all suspicious communications, you'll significantly reduce your risk of falling victim to phishing, smishing, or vishing attacks. Remember, vigilance and caution are your best defenses against these pervasive threats. Seemingly small details can often betray the malicious intent behind a communication, empowering you to protect yourself in an increasingly complex digital landscape.

Staying informed and practicing proactive security measures are crucial to maintaining your online safety and security. Consistent vigilance and awareness remain your strongest weapons in the ongoing battle against cybercrime. Regularly updating your knowledge on the latest techniques and scams will help you stay ahead of the curve and defend against evolving threats. The digital world is constantly changing, and your approach to online security must adapt with it.

Chapter 2: Technical Mechanisms of Phishing Attacks

Having established the importance of recognizing the superficial cues that betray phishing attempts, we now turn to the technical mechanisms that underpin these attacks. Understanding these aspects will empower you to build a more robust defense - moving beyond simply spotting red flags to grasping how these scams are constructed and executed. While we won't get bogged down in overly complex jargon, familiarity with these underlying methods will enhance your ability to protect yourself.

One of the fundamental techniques used in phishing attacks is DNS Spoofing.

DNS SPOOFING

The Domain Name System (DNS) is like the internet's phone book - it translates human-readable domain names (like google.com) into machine-readable IP addresses that computers use to communicate. In a DNS spoofing attack, the attacker manipulates DNS records to redirect users to a malicious website. For example, if you type "yourbank.com" into your browser, a successful spoofing attack could route you to a fraudulent site that looks identical to your bank's legitimate one. This allows the attacker to steal your login credentials and other sensitive information - without you ever realizing you're on a fake website.

The sophistication of this technique can vary. Some attackers may control a compromised DNS server, while others use more subtle methods, such as exploiting vulnerabilities in routers or network devices.

The ability to analyze email headers is another crucial technical skill for identifying fraudulent emails. Email headers contain metadata about an email's journey, including the sender's IP address, the mail servers it passed through, and the date and time it was sent. Examining these headers can reveal inconsistencies or anomalies that suggest a malicious message.

For instance, a mismatch between the sender's email address and their IP address could indicate spoofing. Likewise, unusual routing information or timestamps that don't align with the purported sender's location can raise suspicion.

While analyzing email headers does require some technical know-how, several online tools can simplify the process – helping you gain valuable insights into an email's authenticity.

Malicious links and attachments are at the core of many phishing attacks. Attackers often use URL shortening services to mask the true destination of a link. A shortened URL might appear harmless, but could redirect you to a malicious website designed to steal your information.

Similarly, malicious attachments can carry malware such as keyloggers or ransomware, which can infect your computer and compromise your data. These attachments often seem innocuous—a harmless-looking document, image, or spreadsheet—but once opened, they unleash their destructive payload.

Understanding how these attachments work, even at a high level, improves your ability to assess risk. For example, an unexpected .exe file from an unknown sender should immediately raise a red flag - regardless of the name on the email.

The craft of deceptive emails and messages is a critical component of a successful phishing campaign. Attackers meticulously design these communications to appear legitimate, mirroring the style, tone, and branding of trusted organizations. This includes understanding the target audience—whether a major corporation or a single individual—to tailor the message for maximum impact.

The use of logos, fonts, and language all play a crucial role in creating a sense of authenticity. Sophisticated attacks may even incorporate dynamic content that changes based on the user's location or browser information, further enhancing their credibility and making them harder to distinguish from legitimate communications.

Understanding these design elements helps in spotting a fraudulent email, as even subtle inconsistencies can betray its true nature.

Domain masking is another sophisticated technique often used in phishing attacks. It involves creating a fake domain that closely resembles a legitimate one. Attackers might use a similar-sounding name, a misspelled version of the real domain, or even a different top-level domain (TLD).

This tactic is especially effective on mobile devices with smaller screens, where subtle differences are harder to spot. For example, a phishing email might use "googIe.com" (with an uppercase "I" instead of a lowercase "l") instead of "google.com." These small differences are easy to miss at a glance but reveal malicious intent upon closer inspection.

Social engineering is the art of manipulating individuals into divulging confidential information or performing actions that compromise their security. In phishing attacks, it's often used to create a sense of urgency, fear, or trust - making victims more likely to fall for the scam.

Attackers may pose as legitimate representatives from banks, government agencies, or other trusted organizations to gain the victim's trust. They might also manufacture urgency by claiming immediate action is needed to avoid account suspension or financial loss.

Understanding the psychological principles behind social engineering—such as exploiting trust, fear, and greed—is key to recognizing and resisting these types of attacks.

The technical aspects of phishing attacks are constantly evolving, with attackers developing increasingly sophisticated techniques. Staying informed about the latest trends and threats is critical to protecting yourself.

This includes understanding emerging technologies like artificial intelligence (AI) and machine learning (ML), which are being used both to craft more convincing phishing attacks and to combat them. AI-powered phishing tools can generate highly personalized, targeted emails - making them even harder to identify as fraudulent. At the same time, AI and ML are driving the development of more advanced anti-phishing solutions.

This ongoing arms race between attackers and defenders underscores the dynamic nature of cybersecurity - and the importance of staying vigilant.

Beyond the technical elements, the human factor remains critical. Phishing attacks rely on our tendency to trust, our susceptibility to fear and urgency, and our often-rushed interactions with technology. This makes education and awareness essential components of any comprehensive defense strategy.

Teaching individuals to be cautious, skeptical, and to verify information independently is just as important as understanding the underlying technical mechanisms. This means promoting a culture of security awareness, encouraging healthy skepticism, and providing clear, accessible guidelines for recognizing and responding to phishing attempts.

In summary, understanding the technical mechanisms of phishing attacks—from DNS spoofing and email header analysis to malicious links, deceptive email design, domain masking, and social engineering—is essential to building a strong defense.

But technical knowledge alone isn't enough. It must be paired with an awareness of the psychological tactics attackers use, a commitment to continuous learning, and a culture that prioritizes security awareness.

Only by combining technical proficiency with human awareness can we effectively combat the ever-evolving threat of phishing and protect ourselves in today's complex digital landscape. The battle against cybercrime is ongoing, and staying informed, vigilant, and proactive remains our best defense.

Continuous learning is essential to stay ahead of new techniques and scams. As the digital world continues to change, your approach to online security must evolve with it - embracing a proactive, informed mindset to stay protected.

Chapter 3: Analyzing the Psychology of Social Engineering

Analyzing the psychology of social engineering reveals a fascinating interplay between technological prowess and the exploitation of human vulnerability. While technical skills are essential for crafting sophisticated phishing emails, malicious websites, and other digital traps, the ultimate success of these attacks hinges on manipulating the human element.

Cybercriminals exploit our cognitive biases, emotional responses, and ingrained social behaviors to bypass rational thinking and achieve their malicious goals.

One of the most effective tools in a social engineer's arsenal is **urgency**. A common tactic involves crafting messages that suggest immediate action is required to avoid a negative consequence.

Phishing emails often claim that an account will be suspended, a transaction cancelled, or a payment overdue if the recipient doesn't act immediately. This sense of urgency overrides critical thinking, pushing victims to react impulsively without scrutinizing the message's legitimacy.

Attackers count on the fear of missing out or facing a negative consequence to bypass rational judgment and prompt quick, unthinking action.

The principle of **scarcity** complements urgency. Attackers create a sense that an opportunity or resource is limited or time-sensitive, tapping into our innate desire for exclusivity and fear of missing out. This makes us more likely to act without proper due diligence.

Scarcity tactics work especially well in scams involving limited-time offers, special promotions, or unique opportunities. The promise of exclusivity and limited availability pressures recipients to act quickly - often ignoring warning signs or inconsistencies.

Fear, often coupled with urgency, is another powerful tool in the social engineer's arsenal. Phishing attacks exploit fears of identity theft, financial loss, legal trouble, or even physical harm. These emotionally charged messages bypass logic, creating panic that drives impulsive action.

For example, an email claiming a family member has been in an accident and needs immediate financial help leverages the fear of losing a loved one to provoke an urgent response. Overwhelming emotions response often overshadows critical thinking, causing victims to miss inconsistencies or red flags.

The power of **authority** plays a major role in successful social engineering. Attackers often impersonate figures like government officials, bank representatives, or IT support staff. This tactic taps into our ingrained respect for authority and our tendency to trust those perceived as credible.

For example, an email appearing to come from a government agency can carry significant weight, increasing the chances that a recipient will follow its instructions. Impersonating a trusted authority lends a sense of legitimacy that lowers the victim's skepticism.

Trust is a cornerstone of social engineering. Attackers carefully cultivate it by mimicking the language, tone, and visual style of legitimate organizations. They might use official logos, professional language, and accurate details to create an air of authenticity.

This carefully crafted facade makes it easier to extract sensitive information or manipulate victims into performing specific actions. By building rapport and presenting a friendly, engaging interaction, attackers exploit our natural tendency to help those we trust – or think we do.

Reciprocity is a powerful psychological principle that social engineers frequently exploit. People are more likely to comply with a request if they feel they've received something in return – whether it's a small favor, useful information, or a generous offer.

After receiving something, the recipient may feel obligated to reciprocate, even if it means sharing sensitive information or taking a risky action. This subtle sense of obligation can be remarkably effective in lowering defenses and prompting cooperation.

Liking also plays a crucial role. People are more inclined to trust and comply with individuals they like or feel a connection with. Social engineers may use techniques to build rapport, create familiarity, or establish a personal connection with their targets.

This might involve using friendly language, sharing personal anecdotes, or even tailoring the communication to match the target's interests. By fostering a sense of connection, the attacker makes it easier to bypass skepticism and lower defenses.

Consensus is another subtle but effective technique. People often look to others for cues on how to behave, especially in uncertain situations. Attackers may use testimonials, social proof, or imply that many others have already taken a particular action to influence their target's behavior.

This creates a sense of social pressure, making the victim more likely to comply because it seems like the acceptable course of action. Analyzing successful social engineering campaigns reveals a pattern: a careful blend of these psychological tactics.

For example, the notorious phishing attack targeting Illinois Department of Human Services (IDHS) in 2024 combined urgency ("Your account has been compromised!"), fear ("Your data is at risk!"), and authority ("This message is from IDHS"). The carefully crafted email successfully manipulated many users into divulging their login credentials.

Similarly, the recent rise in smishing attacks - using SMS messages to deliver malicious links - leverages the immediate nature of text messages to create urgent, often panic-inducing responses. The use of seemingly innocuous language, combined with links to what appear to be official websites, exploits the recipient's desire to act quickly and without thinking.

Building resilience against social engineering requires understanding these psychological tactics. By recognizing the underlying manipulative strategies, we can develop a more critical and skeptical approach to unsolicited communications. This includes practicing the following:

- **Verify information independently:** Never rely solely on information provided in a suspicious communication. Contact the organization directly through official channels (website or phone number from a trusted source) to verify any requests for information or actions.

- **Be cautious of urgency:** Don't rush into decisions based on pressure or claims of immediate consequences. Take your time to evaluate the communication carefully.

- **Question authority:** Don't assume that someone claiming to be an authority figure is who they say they are. Verify their identity through official channels.

- **Be wary of requests for personal information:** Legitimate organizations rarely ask for sensitive information via email, text, or phone.

- **Review communications carefully:** Look for typos, grammatical errors, inconsistencies in branding, or suspicious links.

- **Trust your instincts:** If something feels wrong, it probably is.

- **Educate yourself and others:** Stay informed about the latest social engineering tactics and teach friends and family how to protect themselves.

In conclusion, while technical cybersecurity skills are crucial, the human element remains the weakest link in the chain. Understanding the psychological manipulation techniques used by social engineers is paramount to building a robust defense against these ever-evolving threats.

By combining technical proficiency with psychological awareness and a proactive security mindset, we can significantly reduce our vulnerability and protect ourselves in an increasingly complex digital world. The battle against social engineering is ongoing – an evolving process of education, awareness, and critical thinking. The more we grasp the psychological landscape of these attacks, the better equipped we become to safeguard ourselves and those around us.

Chapter 4: Case Studies – Real World Examples of Phishing Attacks

The preceding discussion explored the psychological underpinnings of social engineering attacks, highlighting the manipulative tactics cybercriminals use to exploit human vulnerabilities. Now, we delve into the practical application of these techniques through detailed case studies of real-world phishing, smishing, and vishing attacks. These examples illustrate the diverse methods used, the vulnerabilities exploited, and the potential consequences for victims - underscoring the critical need for vigilance and robust security practices.

CASE STUDY #1: 2024 Snowflake Data Breach

2024 Snowflake data breach. This breach involved unauthorized access to customer cloud environments hosted on Snowflake Inc., a cloud-based data warehousing platform. Attackers exploited stolen credentials obtained via infostealer malware, targeting customers who had not implemented multi-factor authentication (MFA). The breach affected numerous high-profile clients, including AT&T, Ticketmaster, Santander Bank, and Advance Auto Parts, leading to the theft of sensitive data such as personally identifiable information (PII), medical prescriber DEA numbers, and digital event tickets. The attackers, identified as members of the hacking group UNC5537 or Scattered Spider, used the stolen data for extortion, demanding ransoms from affected organizations. This incident underscores the critical importance of enforcing MFA and securing third-party integrations to prevent similar breaches.

CASE STUDY #2: 2024 U.S. Presidential Campaigns

In mid-2024, Iranian hackers affiliated with the Islamic Revolutionary Guard Corps (IRGC), specifically the group known as APT42 (also referred to as Charming Kitten or Mint Sandstorm), launched spear-phishing attacks against individuals associated with both the Trump and Biden presidential campaigns. These attacks utilized compromised email accounts to send malicious links to campaign staffers, aiming to harvest credentials and gain unauthorized access to sensitive campaign information. Notably, the Trump campaign confirmed that it had been successfully breached, with internal documents, including a 271-page vetting report on vice presidential candidate JD Vance, leaked to media outlets such as Politico. The Biden campaign reported that it had been targeted but did not suffer a breach.

CASE STUDY #3: Smishing Attacks Targeting Financial Institutions

Another illustrative example is the widespread use of smishing attacks targeting financial institutions.

Cybercriminals send text messages that appear to come from legitimate banks or credit unions, urging recipients to update their account information, verify a transaction, or respond to a security alert. These messages typically contain links to fraudulent websites designed to mimic the legitimate bank's legitimate site. Unsuspecting victims who click the links are led to pages where they're prompted to enter banking credentials, account numbers, and other sensitive information. This data is then harvested by attackers, enabling them to access victims' accounts and the perpetration of financial fraud. The insidious nature of these attacks lies in their ability to bypass email filters and exploit the immediacy of text messages, capitalizing on the trust associated with SMS communication. The speed and ease with which these messages reach their targets make them particularly effective, and the lack of robust authentication in text messaging leaves them especially vulnerable to this type of attack.

Vishing attacks, which use voice calls, also represent a significant threat. In these attacks, fraudsters pose as representatives from legitimate organizations, such as banks, credit card companies, or government agencies. They contact victims by phone, often using spoofing techniques to disguise their number as that of the organization they're impersonating. These callers then attempt to trick victims into divulging sensitive information, such as banking credentials, social security numbers, or credit card details.

The use of sophisticated voice technology enables scammers to create a believable persona and leverage the perceived authority of the organization they're impersonating. The psychological manipulation relies on a mix of urgency and authority, pressuring the victim to act quickly and trust the caller's claims. Attackers often use scare tactics, suggesting that the victim's account has been compromised or that they're under investigation - creating a sense of panic that overrides rational thinking.

CASE STUDY #4: Vishing Attack Targeting an Elderly Individual

Consider a case study involving a vishing attack targeting an elderly individual. The scammer, impersonating a representative from the victim's bank, claimed the account had been compromised, and that immediate action was needed to prevent significant financial losses. The scammer guided the victim through a series of steps, including providing their account number, PIN, and other personal details - under the guise of verifying their identity and securing their account. Fearing for their financial security and trusting the caller's authority, the victim complied with the instructions, ultimately allowing the scammer to access and drain their bank account. This case underscores the vulnerability of certain demographics, particularly the elderly, who may be more susceptible to the psychological manipulation tactics employed by fraudsters.

These case studies illustrate the diverse tactics employed in phishing, smishing, and vishing attacks, highlighting the creativity and persistence of cybercriminals in exploiting human vulnerabilities. The consequences can range from minor inconveniences to significant financial losses and irreparable damage to reputation and trust. Understanding the common characteristics and patterns of these attacks is crucial in building a strong defense.

Key aspects to focus on include analyzing the sender's information, verifying the authenticity of links and attachments, scrutinizing the language and tone of the communication, and never providing sensitive information through unsolicited channels.

Furthermore, it's essential to recognize that these attacks constantly evolve. Cybercriminals adapt their techniques based on successes and failures, incorporating new technologies and exploiting emerging vulnerabilities. To stay ahead of these threats, continuous education, awareness, and robust security measures are crucial.

Organizations and individuals alike must prioritize cybersecurity training and invest in advanced security solutions to combat the ever-evolving threat landscape.

Regular security audits, strong password management, and multi-factor authentication are crucial steps in mitigating the risk of these attacks.

Moreover, fostering a culture of security awareness within organizations is essential. Employees at all levels must be educated about the various types of phishing attacks and trained to recognize and report suspicious communications. Ultimately, a multi-layered approach - combining technical measures and human awareness - is the most effective way to combat these sophisticated and persistent threats. The ongoing battle against phishing, smishing, and vishing requires constant adaptation and refinement of security strategies to counteract the ingenuity of cybercriminals.

Chapter 5: Email Security Best Practices

Building a robust email security posture is paramount in the fight against phishing attacks. Email remains a primary vector for malicious actors, and neglecting its security leaves you exceptionally vulnerable. This section outlines practical steps you can take to significantly bolster your email security and minimize risk. We'll explore both technical measures and behavioral changes that, when combined, create a formidable defense against phishing attempts.

Two-Factor and Multi-Factor Authentication

First and foremost, **enable two-factor authentication (2FA) or multi-factor authentication (MFA)** on all your email accounts. This seemingly simple step adds an extra layer of security that dramatically reduces the likelihood of unauthorized access. Even if a phisher obtains your password, they'll still need access to your secondary authentication method—a code sent to your phone, a security key, or a biometric scan—to gain entry. Most email providers offer 2FA/MFA, and enabling it should be a top priority. Don't overlook this crucial step - it's often the single most effective measure you can take.

Different providers may offer varying methods for implementing 2FA, so familiarize yourself with your provider's specific instructions. For example,

Google offers several options, including authenticator apps, security keys, and backup codes. Microsoft accounts similarly support a range of 2FA options. Explore these options and choose the method that best suits your needs and technological capabilities. Consider using a dedicated authenticator app for improved security and convenience.

Next, leverage the **email filtering capabilities** offered by your provider. Most email services include spam and junk mail filters designed to identify and quarantine suspicious emails before they reach your inbox. Review and adjust the settings to enhance their effectiveness. Many filters let you customize the level of aggressiveness, enabling you to fine-tune the balance between catching unwanted emails and accidentally blocking legitimate messages. Experiment with different settings to find what works best for your needs.

Understanding how your email filter works - and its limitations - is crucial. While these filters are helpful, they're not foolproof and can sometimes miss malicious emails. Always maintain a critical eye when examining messages, regardless of where they land in your inbox. Furthermore, consider using advanced options such as content filtering, which can scan emails for known malicious content, links, or attachments, effectively blocking messages that may harbor malware.

Beyond the built-in features, many email providers offer **advanced security settings** that you can fine-tune for enhanced protection. Explore your email settings thoroughly. Look for options to block emails from unknown senders, limit the forwarding of your emails, and disable autoresponder functionalities while you're away. These might seem like minor tweaks, but cumulatively, they contribute to a more secure email environment.

Regularly reviewing your email settings ensures that your security measures stay up-to-date and effective against the ever-evolving tactics employed by phishers. Check for updates to your email provider's security features, as they frequently add new tools and capabilities to combat phishing threats. Remember, maintaining a proactive approach to email security is essential.

Password security is an integral component of email security.

Create **strong, unique passwords** for all your email accounts. Avoid using easily guessable passwords like your name, birthday, or common words. A strong password includes a mix of uppercase and lowercase letters, numbers, and symbols. Consider using a password manager to generate and securely store complex passwords for you. This simplifies managing multiple unique passwords without sacrificing security. Password managers encrypt and protect your passwords from unauthorized access. Many also include additional security features, such as two-factor authentication, adding another layer of protection. Always update your passwords regularly - ideally every three months or as recommended by your security guidelines.

In addition to strong passwords, consider using **encrypted email** whenever possible. Encryption scrambles your email content, making it unreadable to anyone except the intended recipient. End-to-end encrypted email services offer the highest level of protection, ensuring your messages remain private throughout the entire transmission process. While not always practical for all communication, prioritizing encryption for sensitive information significantly reduces the risk of interception and compromise. Several encrypted email services are available, each offering varying levels of security and features. Explore your options and choose the service that best aligns with your needs and technical proficiency. Remember, encryption is just one layer of security - maintaining good email hygiene and awareness remains crucial.

Avoid using public Wi-Fi to access sensitive email accounts. Public Wi-Fi networks are notoriously insecure, making your email vulnerable to interception by malicious actors. If you must use public Wi-Fi, consider using a VPN (Virtual Private Network) to encrypt your internet traffic and shield your email from prying eyes. VPNs create a secure tunnel for your online activities, protecting your data from unauthorized access. Choosing a reputable VPN provider is essential to ensure your privacy and security. Before connecting to any public Wi-Fi, make sure you understand the security risks involved.

Regularly **review your email inbox for any suspicious activity.** Watch for unsolicited emails, unexpected attachments, unusual login attempts, or changes to your email settings. Familiarize yourself with common phishing indicators such as poor grammar, generic greetings, suspicious links, and requests for personal information. If you notice anything suspicious, take immediate action: change your passwords, report the incident to your email provider, and take any other necessary steps to protect your accounts. Proactive monitoring can help detect potential attacks early and minimize their impact.

When in doubt, **verify the sender's identity** *before* responding to emails or clicking links. Check the sender's email address carefully. Does it look legitimate? Has the sender contacted you before? Watch for inconsistencies in the email address like misspellings or unusual characters.

Hover over any links before clicking to see where they actually lead. If the link's destination doesn't match the sender's claim, it's a strong indication of a phishing attempt.

Never hesitate to contact the supposed sender directly through a known legitimate channel to verify the email's authenticity - even if you're initially unsure. Confirming the legitimacy of the communication directly with the organization is often the best way to avoid falling victim to a phishing attempt.

Never open attachments from unknown or untrusted sources.

Attachments can harbor malware that infects your computer and steals your information. If you receive an attachment from an unknown sender, don't open it. Even if the sender is known, exercise caution if the attachment is unexpected or seems suspicious. When in doubt, always contact the sender before opening an attachment. Malicious attachments come in many forms - documents, images, and executable files alike. Treat each attachment cautiously and critically. Your computer's security depends heavily on your vigilance when managing and accessing email attachments.

Never provide sensitive information in response to unsolicited emails.

Legitimate organizations will never ask for personal details like passwords, credit card numbers, or social security numbers via email. If you receive such a request, it's almost certainly a phishing attempt. Report the suspicious email to your email provider and contact the organization directly to verify the request's legitimacy. Never assume an email is authentic. Always exercise caution and confirm details through official, secure channels. This simple step can prevent significant financial and personal risks.

By implementing these email security best practices, you significantly reduce your vulnerability to phishing attacks. Remember, a multi-layered approach - combining technical safeguards with informed user behavior - is the most effective way to protect yourself. Stay vigilant, stay informed, and stay safe. Cybersecurity is a continuous process of learning and adapting to ever-evolving attacker tactics. Staying updated on the latest threats and adopting new defenses is key to your overall online safety. Regularly updating and adjusting your email security protocols is fundamental in this ongoing cyber battle.

Chapter 6: Securing Your Mobile Devices

Your mobile device - whether a smartphone or tablet - is an extension of your digital life. It holds personal data, financial information, and access to countless online services. This makes it a prime target for smishing attacks – phishing scams delivered via text message. Protecting your mobile devices is crucial to preventing these attacks and safeguarding your sensitive information. While many email security principles apply equally to mobile security, there are specific vulnerabilities and protective measures unique to mobile devices that require attention.

The first line of defense is robust anti-malware software. Just like your computer, your smartphone or tablet is vulnerable to viruses and malware that can compromise your security and allow attackers to intercept your data. Make sure you have a reputable anti-malware app installed and regularly updated. Many free options offer strong protection against various mobile threats, while premium versions often provide more comprehensive features and faster updates. Choose a provider with a good track record of identifying and neutralizing malware. Review user feedback and security reports before installing any software. Don't rely solely on your device's built-in security; a dedicated anti-malware app adds an essential extra layer of protection against evolving threats. Consider enabling automatic updates for your anti-malware app to ensure your device benefits from the latest threat detection.

Regularly updating your operating system (OS) is another fundamental step. OS updates often include security patches that fix vulnerabilities exploited by malicious actors. Ignoring these updates leaves your device exposed. Enable automatic updates whenever possible, so your device can install security patches without manual intervention. However, it's advisable to back up your data before major OS updates, as unforeseen issues can sometimes occur. Regularly checking for and installing updates is a proactive measure that can significantly enhance your mobile security. Be mindful of the notification messages from your OS provider; these often indicate the availability of crucial updates that address recently discovered security flaws. By keeping your OS current, you minimize the risk of exploitation through known vulnerabilities.

Beyond software, your device's built-in security features are vital. These often include passcodes, fingerprint recognition, or facial recognition. Activating these safeguards adds significant protection against unauthorized access. A strong passcode - incorporating a mix of uppercase and lowercase letters, numbers, and symbols - creates a strong barrier against brute-force attacks. Regularly changing your passcode strengthens your security posture, reducing the risk of unauthorized access even if someone manages to obtain your previous one.

Evaluate the various biometric options offered by your device; facial recognition and fingerprint scanners can provide added convenience while boosting security. However, keep in mind the limitations of biometric authentication - these methods can be susceptible to spoofing in certain circumstances. A strong passcode remains a valuable supplemental measure.

App stores are convenient but can also be breeding grounds for malicious applications. Always download apps exclusively from official app stores like Google Play Store for Android devices or the Apple App Store for iOS devices.

These platforms have review processes to filter out malicious apps, although they're not foolproof. Read reviews and check the developer's information before downloading an app. Be wary of apps that request excessive permissions - especially those that seem unnecessary for the app's functionality. Check the app's privacy policy to understand how your data will be handled. Consider the reputation of the developer: are they well-known and trustworthy, or an obscure, lesser-known entity?

Always exercise caution when installing apps, even if they're recommended by others. Verify the app's legitimacy and purpose before granting access to sensitive data or features on your device. Avoid downloading or installing apps from unofficial sources, as these lack the rigorous vetting processes of official app stores and may harbor malicious code.

Beware of suspicious SMS messages. Smishing attempts often involve links or attachments. Never click on links or open attachments in messages from unknown senders. Even if the sender appears familiar, be cautious if the message is unexpected or if the request seems unusual. If you're uncertain about a message's legitimacy, verify the sender's identity through a known, secure channel—such as a phone call to a confirmed number or an email sent to the legitimate organization, not a link provided in the SMS message.

Never reply to messages requesting personal information, such as banking details, passwords, or social security numbers. Legitimate organizations will rarely, if ever, ask for such sensitive data via SMS. If you receive a suspicious message, report it to your mobile carrier and the relevant authorities. Proactive vigilance and critical analysis of SMS messages are crucial in thwarting smishing attempts.

Another crucial aspect of mobile security is keeping your device software up-to-date. This includes not only the operating system but also individual apps. Outdated apps often contain security vulnerabilities that can be exploited by malicious actors. Enable automatic updates for your apps whenever possible, but also check for updates manually from time to time, as some apps may not automatically update for various reasons.

Regularly review your app permissions to ensure that apps only have access to the data they truly need. Revoke unnecessary permissions to enhance both your privacy and security. This is a critical step in controlling what data apps can access and preventing potential misuse. By keeping your apps updated and permissions in check, you significantly reduce the risk of being exploited and strengthen your device's overall security.

Finally, be mindful of your surroundings when using your mobile device. Avoid using your phone in public places where someone might be able to observe your screen or interactions. Be cautious of public Wi-Fi networks; these can be easily compromised and used by attackers to intercept your data. If you must use public Wi-Fi, use a VPN to encrypt your internet traffic.

Use your device's location services carefully - know which apps have access to your precise location, and selectively enable or disable tracking as needed. The more aware you are of your surroundings and the risks of public spaces, the better you can protect yourself and your devices from potential attacks. This vigilance complements other mobile security measures and strengthens your overall security posture.

In conclusion, securing your mobile devices requires a multi-faceted approach. By diligently installing and updating anti-malware software, regularly updating your operating system and apps, enabling strong device security features, downloading apps from trusted sources, exercising caution with SMS messages, and being mindful of your surroundings, you can significantly reduce your vulnerability to smishing attacks and protect your valuable personal information.

Remember, vigilance and proactive security measures are your strongest allies in the ongoing battle against cyber threats. Staying informed about the latest threats and adopting new protective measures is crucial to staying ahead of malicious actors and ensuring the continued security of your digital life.

Chapter 7: Password Management Strategies

The foundation of a robust online security posture rests on a critical element often overlooked: *password management.*

In the face of sophisticated phishing attacks, using weak or easily guessable passwords is akin to leaving your front door unlocked—an open invitation to disaster. This section delves into essential strategies for safeguarding your digital identity through effective password management. The goal isn't simply to create passwords, but to create a system that's both secure and manageable – one capable of withstanding the ever-evolving tactics of cybercriminals.

The first principle is creating strong, unique passwords for each online account. The days of using the same password across multiple platforms are long gone. This practice is a recipe for catastrophic data breaches. If one account is compromised, a hacker gains access to all accounts secured with that single password. This domino effect can lead to identity theft, financial loss, and major disruption to both your personal and professional life.

So, what constitutes a strong password? The simplest answer is complexity. Avoid simple sequences of numbers or letters, such as "123456" or "password." Instead, aim for passwords that are long and combine uppercase and lowercase letters, numbers, and symbols. A password of at least 12 characters is recommended - but the longer, the better. For example, a strong password might look like this: "P@$$wOrd!2024." Notice the mix of uppercase and lowercase letters, numbers, and symbols. This password is considerably harder to crack than a shorter, simpler one.

However, remembering dozens or even hundreds of unique, complex passwords is an impractical - even impossible - task for most people. That's where password managers become invaluable tools. These sophisticated software applications securely store and manage your passwords. They generate strong, unique passwords for each account and encrypt them to protect against unauthorized access. Many reputable password managers also offer features like multi-factor authentication (MFA), adding an extra layer of security by requiring a second verification step beyond just your password.

Choosing the right password manager requires careful consideration. Look for established, reputable providers with a proven track record in security and privacy. Read user reviews and check independent security audits before making your choice. Consider features like auto-fill - which seamlessly enters your login credentials - and cross-platform compatibility so you can access your passwords across all your devices. It's also helpful to pick a password manager that offers security alerts, notifying you of potential breaches or suspicious activity on your accounts.

Beyond creating and managing strong passwords, maintaining good password hygiene is equally critical. This includes regularly changing your passwords, especially for accounts containing sensitive information like banking details or email. Avoid predictable patterns when updating passwords - for example, simply adding a number to your old password is easy to guess. Instead, use your password manager to generate entirely new, unique passwords.

Furthermore, avoid using personal information such as your birthday, pet's name, or address in your passwords. These details easy for attackers to guess, especially if they've gathered information about you online. Never share your passwords with anyone, no matter who they claim to be. Legitimate organizations will never ask for your passwords via email, text message, or phone call.

Regularly reviewing your password list and updating any weak passwords is a crucial part of good password hygiene. Your password manager will often flag weak or duplicated passwords, making it easier to identify and fix security risks. Consider scheduling regular password reviews - perhaps every three months or so - to ensure that your passwords stay strong and unique.

The practice of password reuse is another common pitfall that seriously compromises security. Using the same password for multiple accounts increases the risk of a catastrophic breach. If one account is compromised, a hacker gains access to all accounts using that password. Password managers eliminate this risk by generating unique passwords for every account.

In addition to using a password manager, consider employing multi-factor authentication (MFA) whenever it's available. MFA requires multiple forms of authentication to access an account - this could be a password, a code sent to your phone, or a biometric scan. Adding MFA significantly reduces the risk of unauthorized access, even if your password is compromised. It creates a much stronger barrier against potential attackers.

Finally, educate yourself about phishing scams and social engineering tactics. Phishing attempts often try to trick you into revealing your passwords or other sensitive information.

By understanding how these scams work, you can spot them more easily and avoid becoming a victim. Being vigilant and skeptical of unexpected emails, texts, or phone calls can make a big difference in protecting your passwords and overall online security.

In conclusion, effective password management is a multifaceted process involving the creation of strong, unique passwords, the use of a reputable password manager, good password hygiene practices, and the use of multi-factor authentication whenever possible. By following these strategies, you significantly reduce your vulnerability to phishing attacks and protect your sensitive personal information in today's complex digital landscape. It's an investment in your personal security that pays dividends in peace of mind and the protection of your digital assets. Remember, security is an ongoing process - and staying informed about the latest threats and best practices is crucial for safeguarding your online presence.

Chapter 8: Safe Online Behavior and Practices

B eyond strong passwords and robust password management systems, your online behavior significantly influences your susceptibility to phishing attacks. A careless click, a moment of inattention, or a lapse in judgment can expose you to sophisticated scams designed to steal your personal data and financial resources. This section emphasizes the proactive measures you can take to minimize your risk and create a safer online experience.

One of the most crucial aspects of safe online behavior is verifying the authenticity of websites. Before entering any personal information, take a moment to critically examine the website's URL. Look for inconsistencies or misspellings that could indicate a fraudulent site. Legitimate websites typically have secure connections, denoted by "https" at the beginning of the URL and a padlock icon in the address bar. Hover your mouse over links before clicking to see the actual destination URL - this helps prevent redirects to malicious sites. Be wary of websites with generic or unprofessional designs, as they often signal a lack of legitimacy.

Legitimate organizations will rarely request sensitive information via email. Always treat such requests with extreme skepticism. Never reply directly to emails asking for personal information. Instead, navigate to the official website of the organization and contact them through established channels. Check the sender's email address carefully - phishing emails often use similar-looking, yet subtly different, addresses to deceive recipients. For instance, a fraudulent message might appear to come from "paypaI@example.com" instead of the legitimate "paypal@paypal.com".

Avoid clicking on links embedded within suspicious emails or text messages. These links frequently redirect users to malicious websites designed to steal login credentials, credit card information, or other sensitive data. If you must access a link from an email, it's safer to type the website address manually into your browser rather than clicking the provided link.

Downloading attachments from unknown or untrusted sources presents a significant security risk. Malicious attachments can contain viruses, malware, or other harmful code that may infect your computer and compromise your data. Always exercise caution when opening email attachments, especially those from unknown senders or with unexpected file extensions. If you're unsure of an attachment's legitimacy, it's safer to err on the side of caution and avoid opening it. Use reputable antivirus software to scan suspicious attachments before opening them.

Similarly, be wary of unexpected phone calls requesting personal information. Legitimate organizations rarely initiate contact by phone to ask for sensitive data. If you receive a suspicious call from someone claiming to represent a bank, credit card company, or other organization, hang up immediately and contact the organization directly using their official contact information to verify the call's authenticity. Never provide your personal information to anyone who contacted you unsolicited.

The pervasive use of public Wi-Fi networks presents another area of concern for online security. While convenient, public Wi-Fi is notoriously insecure, making it an easy target for cybercriminals. Avoid accessing sensitive information - such as online banking or email – when connected to these networks. If you must use public Wi-Fi, use a virtual private network (VPN) to encrypt your internet traffic and shield your data from prying eyes. VPNs create a secure tunnel between your device and the internet, making it much more difficult for hackers to intercept your data. When selecting a VPN, choose a reputable provider with a strong track record in security and privacy.

Social engineering attacks exploit human psychology to manipulate individuals into revealing sensitive information. These attacks come in many forms, including phishing emails that appear to be from trusted sources, phone calls from people posing as tech support, or even in-person interactions. To protect yourself against social engineering attacks, it's crucial to remain vigilant and skeptical - always verify any unexpected requests before providing personal details. Never feel pressured to act quickly or share information you're uncomfortable giving.

Staying informed about the latest phishing scams and social engineering techniques is vital to maintaining robust online security. Subscribe to security newsletters, follow reputable cybersecurity experts on social media, and regularly review best practices. Familiarity with common phishing tactics can significantly improve your ability to recognize and avoid these attacks.

Understanding the psychology behind phishing attacks is also crucial. These emails and messages often exploit emotions like urgency, fear, or trust to pressure victims into acting impulsively. Recognizing these emotional triggers helps you assess the legitimacy of suspicious communications more effectively. For example, messages demanding immediate action or threatening negative consequences are classic signs of a phishing attempt.

Always pause and analyze the message before reacting.

Regularly updating your software and operating systems is an often overlooked yet crucial aspect of online security. Software updates frequently contain security patches that address known vulnerabilities that could be exploited by cybercriminals. Keeping your software up-to-date minimizes the risk of infections and compromises. Similarly, enable automatic updates for your antivirus software and operating system to ensure that you're consistently protected against the latest threats.

Educate your family and friends about phishing attacks and safe online practices. By sharing your knowledge and empowering others, you contribute to a safer online environment for everyone. A collective understanding of online security risks can dramatically reduce the overall vulnerability to these attacks. Discussing safe online behaviors within your social circle can create a stronger, more resilient community against phishing attempts.

In conclusion, safe online behavior is a crucial component of comprehensive phishing protection. By combining vigilance, skepticism, and the adoption of safe practices, you significantly reduce your vulnerability to these attacks.

Remember, online security is an ongoing process; continuous learning and adaptation are essential for navigating the ever-evolving digital landscape. Proactively adopting the strategies outlined in this section will boost your online safety and give you peace of mind in today's complex digital world. By staying informed, attentive, and proactive, you can greatly reduce your risk of falling victim to phishing attacks.

Remember, your online security isn't just a tech issue; it's about informed behavior and mindful engagement with the digital world.

Chapter 9: Recognizing and Reporting Suspicious Websites

Building upon the strategies we've already covered for avoiding phishing attempts, we now dive into the crucial skill of recognizing and reporting suspicious websites. These sites often act as the final stop for phishing campaigns, aiming to steal your personal information or sneak malware onto your devices. Knowing how to spot these red flags and reporting them is essential for keeping yourself safe online.

The first line of defense is a careful examination of the website's address, also known as the URL. It's an easy detail to overlook, but many phishing sites use subtle variations to mimic legitimate ones. Pay close attention to the spelling – a single misplaced letter, an extra character, or a slightly altered domain name (like "gooogle.com" instead of "google.com") can be clear signs of a fraudulent site. These small changes are easy to miss if you're not looking closely, and they can trick you into handing over sensitive data to the wrong hands.

Beyond simple misspellings, phishing websites often use entirely different domain names that sound remarkably similar to legitimate ones. For instance, a phishing site targeting a popular online retailer might use a domain name like "amaz0n.com" or "am4zon.co.uk," relying on visual similarity to trick unsuspecting users. Always double-check the URL against the official website's address you know to be legitimate - either from a bookmark or by typing it directly into your browser's address bar. Avoid clicking on links embedded in emails or text messages; this one precaution alone can protect you from countless potential security breaches.

Next, examine the website's security certificate. Legitimate websites usually employ Secure Sockets Layer (SSL) or Transport Layer Security (TLS) protocols, which encrypt the communication between your browser and the server. The presence of SSL/TLS is indicated by "https" at the beginning of the URL and a padlock icon usually found in the browser's address bar. However, keep in mind that malicious websites can sometimes fraudulently display this padlock icon – so visual confirmation alone is insufficient.

Clicking the padlock icon should reveal detailed information about the website's security certificate, including the name of the issuing authority and the validity period. If the certificate name doesn't match the website's URL, or if the certificate is expired or self-signed (meaning it wasn't issued by a trusted certificate authority), that's a serious red flag. These inconsistencies suggest the website may not be what it claims to be and should prompt immediate caution.

Visual inspection of the website itself can offer further clues. Legitimate sites from established organizations typically have a professional, consistent design and are free from grammatical errors or obvious spelling mistakes.

Inconsistent branding or low-quality design should raise immediate suspicion. Take a close look at the website's overall aesthetics - is the layout professional, or does it appear hastily constructed and amateurish? Do the images and logos appear authentic, or are they blurry, pixelated, or otherwise suspicious? Do the fonts and color schemes match those of the legitimate organization's official website? These details may seem trivial, but they can reveal major flaws in the site's legitimacy.

Furthermore, carefully scrutinize the website's content for inconsistencies or inaccuracies. Watch for grammatical errors, spelling mistakes, and awkward phrasing – common signs of a hastily created phishing site. Genuine organizations typically invest in professional content creation, while fraudulent sites often lack that level of attention to detail.

Furthermore, verify the contact information provided on the website. Does the email address, phone number, or physical address match that of the legitimate organization? Any discrepancies should raise serious concerns.

Beyond visual cues, pay attention to the website's behavior. Is it requesting an excessive amount of personal information? Legitimate organizations only ask for what's necessary for a specific transaction or interaction. If the website demands unnecessary details, that's a major red flag. Does it use aggressive tactics to solicit your personal information - like creating a false sense of urgency or threatening consequences if you don't comply? These high-pressure strategies are common with phishing attempts. Remember, genuine organizations rarely resort to such tactics.

Another critical element is how the website interacts with your browser. Legitimate websites generally don't bombard you with excessive pop-up windows or intrusive advertisements. An flood of pop-ups or distracting advertisements should be seen as a warning sign.

Additionally, watch for websites that try to download files or software automatically without your explicit permission. This behavior is a clear sign of potential malicious intent.

If you encounter a website showing any of these suspicious signs, it's crucial to act immediately. Don't provide any personal information or engage further. Close the website immediately and clear your browser's history and cache to remove any trace of your interaction.

Reporting suspicious websites is just as important as identifying them. This crucial step helps protect others from falling victim to the same scams. You can report suspicious websites to your internet service provider (ISP), using their designated channels for reporting phishing or malicious sites. Many ISPs have dedicated forms or email addresses for this purpose. Contacting your ISP is essential - they can take action to block access to the malicious site and prevent further victims.

Reporting suspicious websites to law enforcement agencies is another vital step. Many jurisdictions have dedicated cybercrime units that investigate online fraud and cyberattacks. The reporting process may involve providing the website's URL along with supporting evidence, like screenshots or email headers. Law enforcement can then investigate the website's operations, trace the perpetrators, and pursue legal action.

You can also report suspicious websites to the relevant authorities in the website's alleged host country. Many nations have dedicated cybercrime centers or specific agencies that handle these cases. Finding the appropriate authority often means researching the website's domain registration information, which can reveal where the server hosting the malicious website is located. These authorities have the tools and resources to investigate and bring the responsible parties to justice.

In addition to formal reporting channels, consider notifying the web hosting provider. Most reputable hosts have strict policies against malicious content and offer ways to report suspicious websites. Sharing details like the URL and why you believe the website is malicious can help get it taken down.

Websites dedicated to collecting reports on phishing and malicious websites can also be invaluable. They aggregate user reports and provide valuable data to cybersecurity researchers and law enforcement. Contributing your report helps strengthen the collective fight against online fraud and improves safety for everyone.

Remember, proactively identifying and reporting suspicious websites is a shared responsibility. By carefully examining websites before interacting and reporting suspicious activity, you help create a safer online environment for everyone. The steps outlined here, combined with the earlier strategies, form a strong defense against phishing and other online threats. Staying vigilant and informed is your first line of protection against the ever-evolving landscape of online fraud.

Chapter 10: Identifying Vishing Calls – Red Flags and Warning Signs

Vishing, a blend of "voice" and "phishing," is a significant and evolving threat in the digital landscape. Unlike phishing emails or smishing text messages, vishing uses the immediacy and personal touch of a phone call to trick victims into revealing sensitive information. The human voice - with its inflection and emotional nuance - can be a powerful tool for deception, making vishing attacks especially effective. Understanding the tactics vishing scammers use is crucial for building strong defenses.

One of the most common tactics is impersonation. Vishing scammers often pose as representatives from trusted institutions like banks, government agencies, or tech support companies. They might claim your bank account has been compromised, there's an issue with your tax return, or your computer is infected with malware. Their goal is to create urgency and fear, pushing you to act quickly without thinking critically. These calls often begin with a pre-recorded message that sounds official and authoritative, followed by a live operator who engages you in conversation. This transition creates an illusion of legitimacy, making the deception even more convincing.

The sense of urgency is a key element in many vishing attacks. Scammers often use phrases like "Your account has been compromised, and we need to act immediately," or "We've detected suspicious activity and need your information to secure your account." These statements are crafted to bypass your critical thinking and push you into immediate action. They prey on your fear of financial loss or legal trouble, compelling you to provide information without hesitation. Remember, legitimate institutions rarely deliver urgent or sensitive information over the phone without prior, established contact.

Emotional manipulation is another powerful tool in the visher's arsenal. They may exploit your empathy by pretending to be in distress - claiming to be a victim of a crime or experiencing a personal crisis. They might also tap into your guilt, suggesting you owe money or have caused harm to someone else. By targeting your emotions, they bypass your rational thinking and make you more vulnerable to their requests. These emotional appeals are often paired with impersonation, creating a compelling narrative designed to overwhelm your critical judgment.

Identifying these deceptive tactics requires a high degree of awareness and critical thinking. One of the most effective defenses is to stay skeptical of unsolicited calls - especially those asking for sensitive information. Legitimate institutions rarely request login credentials, bank account details, or Social Security numbers over the phone. If you receive such a call, immediately question its legitimacy. Don't hesitate to ask probing questions, verify the caller's identity through independent means, and request a callback number from the official website or contact information you already trust.

Never share personal information unless you've independently confirmed who you're speaking with.

Let's look at some real-world examples to illustrate these deceptive techniques. Imagine receiving a call from someone claiming to be a representative from your bank. They inform you of suspicious transactions on your account and say they need your password to verify your identity. This is a classic vishing tactic, aimed at exploiting your fear of financial loss. A legitimate bank will never ask for your password over the phone - they'll use secure alternatives, like sending a verification code via text or email.

Another example involves a call from someone claiming to be from the IRS. They tell you that you owe a significant amount in taxes and must pay immediately to avoid legal consequences. This tactic relies on both impersonation and manufactured urgency. The IRS rarely contacts individuals by phone to demand immediate payment. They typically communicate through mail, with official notices that include clear instructions and detailed information - never pressure for instant payments.

Consider a scenario where a caller poses as a tech support representative. They claim your computer is infected with malware and say they need remote access to fix the problem. This tactic preys on your fear of data loss or system compromise. Legitimate tech support companies don't randomly call you about computer problems. They work through scheduled appointments or request to customer-initiated requests - never through unsolicited calls demanding immediate action.

Here's a checklist of warning signs to watch for when receiving unexpected calls:

- **Unsolicited calls:** Legitimate institutions rarely initiate contact without prior arrangement.

- **Requests for personal information:** Be cautious if asked for passwords, credit card numbers, Social Security numbers, or other sensitive data.

- **Urgency and panic:** Calls that try to create a sense of panic or urgency are often deceptive.

- **Impersonation of authority figures:** Scammers often pose as bank representatives, government officials, or tech support personnel.

- **Aggressive or threatening language:** Legitimate organizations rarely use aggressive or threatening tactics.

- **Unusual phrasing or grammatical errors:** Poorly written scripts or strange phrasing can indicate a fraudulent call.

- **Unusual phone number:** Treat calls from unexpected or unfamiliar numbers with caution.

- **Requests for remote access:** Be extremely cautious if asked to grant remote access to your computer or mobile device.

- **Unverified Caller ID:** Don't trust Caller ID alone - spoofing technology makes it easy for scammers to disguise their numbers.

- **Unexpected payment requests:** Be wary of any call requesting immediate or unconventional payment methods.

To further protect yourself from vishing attacks, consider these preventative measures:

- **Never provide sensitive information over the phone unless you've independently verified the caller's identity.** Use official contact details from the organization's website or other trusted sources to confirm who you are speaking with.

- **Hang up on suspicious calls.** Don't engage or share any information.

- **Report suspicious calls to the appropriate authorities.** This helps warn others and supports investigations into fraudulent activity.

- **Familiarize yourself with common vishing tactics.** Knowing what to expect makes it easier to spot and avoid scams.

- **Keep your contact information up to date.** Make sure official contact details are correct and accessible - this helps organizations reach you if there's a genuine emergency.

- **Utilize call-blocking and identification apps.** These tools help you screen calls and flag potential scams.

- **Educate yourself and others.** Awareness is your first line of defense against vishing and other social engineering attacks.

The prevalence of vishing demands a proactive approach to personal digital security. By understanding the tactics scammers use and adopting the preventative measures we've discussed, you can greatly reduce your vulnerability to these attacks.

Remember, vigilance and critical thinking are your best weapons against vishing. Stay informed, remain skeptical, and never hesitate to question the legitimacy of any unsolicited call requesting sensitive information. The consequences of falling victim to a vishing attack can be severe, making proactive protection essential. By combining caution, verification, and reporting, you not only lower your own risk but also contribute to a safer online community.

Chapter 11: Techniques for Handling Suspicious Calls

Handling a suspicious phone call requires a calm, assertive approach. While the immediate instinct might be to panic - especially if the caller uses aggressive tactics or tries to create a sense of urgency - reacting impulsively often leads to giving away the very information the scammer wants. The key is to stay in control, gather details, and verify everything independently before taking any action.

Resist the Pressure

The first crucial step is to resist the pressure. Scammers count on fear and anxiety to push you into quick decisions. Take a deep breath and consciously slow your response. Don't rush to confirm any details or share personal information. Remember, legitimate organizations won't pressure you to disclose sensitive data on the spot. They'll understand your need for verification and won't be offended by a cautious approach.

Next, politely but firmly ask for the caller's name and organization. If they're genuinely representing a legitimate entity, they should be able to provide this information without hesitation. Be cautious of vague or evasive responses - many scammers will offer only a generic title or department to avoid specifics. Insist on a clear, verifiable identity. If they refuse or dodge the question, it's a strong indicator of a fraudulent call.

Ask for a Callback Number

The next step is to ask for a callback number - but it must be independently verifiable. Never rely on the number provided by the caller. Instead, look up the official contact information of the organization they claim to represent, usually through their official website or a trusted directory. Once you have the correct contact number, politely end the current call and reach out to the organization directly using the verified contact information. This simple step serves as a crucial verification process, helping you avoid sharing sensitive information with potential scammers.

Scrutinize the Details

It's equally important to scrutinize the details of their claims. Scammers often rely on generic phrases or outdated information, counting on the fact that you may not remember the exact details of your accounts or transactions. If the caller references specifics that are vague or incorrect, it could be a sign of fraud. Legitimate organizations will have accurate, up-to-date information at hand - any inconsistencies suggest a potential scam. For example, if a supposed bank representative calls about a transaction, ask for the exact amount and date of the transaction. If they hesitate or give incorrect information, end the call.

Once you've independently verified the caller's identity and details, you can decide whether to continue the conversation. However, even if the organization appears legitimate, stay cautious about sharing sensitive information over the phone. Legitimate institutions rarely ask for personal data like passwords, credit card numbers, or Social Security numbers by telephone. They typically use secure methods such as email, registered mail, or in-person interactions. If they do ask for sensitive data, be highly suspicious.

Be Firm and Hang Up Immediately

While polite firmness is generally the best approach, some scammers may become aggressive or threatening. If the call turns abusive, hang up immediately. Do not engage with their behavior. If possible, record the number and report the incident to the appropriate authorities. This is especially important if they're threatening legal action or financial penalties – classic scare tactics used to create fear and pressure you into acting quickly. Never give in to that pressure.

If you're unsure whether a call is legitimate, it's always safer to err on the side of caution and end the call. There's no penalty for being cautious – but the consequences of falling for a vishing scam can be serious, including financial loss, identity theft, and emotional distress. Remember: your safety and security come first.

Let's explore some specific scenarios and how to address them effectively:

Scenario 1: A supposed bank representative calls, claiming there's been fraudulent activity on your account.

Your response: "Thank you for calling. However, before I disclose any information, could I please have your name and employee ID? I would also appreciate a callback number. I'll verify this information independently via my bank's official website before continuing."

Next Steps: Hang up. Visit your bank's official website or use a trusted phone number from your bank statement or official documents to confirm the claim. Never call the number provided by the potential scammer.

Scenario 2: Someone claiming to be from the IRS demands immediate tax payment.

Your response: "I understand your concern regarding taxes. However, I need to verify your identity. Could you please provide your name, employee ID, and a callback number for an official IRS representative? I'll call you back after verifying your information through the official IRS website."

Next Steps: Hang up. Visit the official IRS website to find the correct contact information and independently verify the claim. Never provide financial or personal details over the phone unless you've confirmed the caller's identity through official channels. Remember, the IRS typically communicates by mail - not phone calls.

Scenario 3: A tech support representative claims your computer is infected and needs immediate remote access.

Your response: "Thank you for your concern about my computer. Before granting remote access, I'll need to verify your identity. Could you provide your name, company ID, and a callback number? I'll contact you back through an independently verified number from your company's official website."

Next Steps: Hang up. Do not allow any remote access unless you have independently contacted the tech support provider and scheduled an appointment. Legitimate tech support companies do not call out of the blue demanding immediate remote access.

Scenario 4: A caller claims to be a relative in distress, urgently requesting money.

Your Response: "I'm concerned to hear this. Before sending any money, I need to make sure everything is truly okay. Could you please provide some details and a way to independently verify your identity? I'll reach out through your known contact information to confirm the situation before moving forward."

Next Steps: Contact other family members or friends to verify the claim before sending any money. Scammers often prey on emotion, so it's essential to pause and confirm the facts before taking any actions that could have financial consequences.

Remember, these are just examples. Every suspicious call should be handled with caution, and you should never hesitate to question the caller's motives or requests. By following these guidelines and using your critical thinking skills, you can greatly reduce your risk of falling victim to a vishing attack. Staying calm, verifying information, and reporting suspicious calls are essential steps in protecting yourself in today's increasingly complex digital world. A little effort spent on verification is far less costly than the potential consequences of falling for a scam.

Chapter 12: Protecting Your Phone and Voicemail

Protecting your phone and voicemail is crucial in the fight against vishing. These devices are prime targets for scammers, offering a direct line to potential victims. While we've covered how to handle suspicious calls, taking proactive steps to secure your phone and voicemail is just as important – if not more. This requires a multi-layered approach that includes both software safeguards and behavioral changes.

One of the most effective preventative measures is enabling call screening features available on most modern smartphones. These tools let you pre-screen calls, identifying potential spam or robocalls before they even reach your ear. Many operating systems, like Android and iOS, include built-in spam call identification services that use community reports to flag suspicious numbers.

Activating these features serves as a first line of defense, significantly reducing the chances of unwanted scam calls. Plus, many phone providers offer similar call-blocking and identification services as part of their plans. Check your phone's settings and your provider's options to make sure you're fully leveraging these protections.

Don't forget to regularly review and update your blocked numbers list - you might be surprised how many unwanted numbers accumulate over time. Consider setting up alerts for new blocked calls so you stay informed.

Beyond call screening, actively blocking known scam numbers is another essential step. If you receive a suspicious call, immediately add the number to your blocked list. Most smartphones make this easy – usually through the phone's call log or settings.

Remember, scammers often spoof their numbers, so the number you see might not be their actual number. While you can't always stop spoofing, blocking known scam numbers still helps cut down the number of fraudulent calls you receive. Plus, many phone apps offer advanced call-blocking features that automatically block numbers flagged by community reports as likely scams. These apps can often catch and block suspicious calls before they even ring on your phone.

Regularly updating your phone's operating system and apps is crucial. These updates often include security patches that fix vulnerabilities scammers could exploit.

Outdated software leaves your phone open to potential attacks, making it easier for scammers to gain access or compromise your data. This simple step is one of the most effective ways to boost your phone's security. Whenever possible, enable automatic updates to keep your device running the latest – and safest - software.

When it comes to voicemail security, choosing and maintaining a strong, unique password is essential. Avoid easily guessed passwords like your birthdate, pet's name, or sequential numbers. Instead, use a complex password that includes uppercase and lowercase letters, numbers, and symbols. A password manager can help generate and securely store strong, unique passwords for all your accounts - including voicemail.

Regularly changing your voicemail password helps minimize the risk of unauthorized access. This simple habit is a key part of maintaining a strong security posture. Many voicemail systems also offer additional security features, such as two-factor authentication, that can further strengthen your account's protection. Explore the options available on your provider's platform and utilize these enhanced security measures.

Think of your voicemail password as another crucial layer of defense - just as important as your online banking or social media passwords. Treating it with the same level of care and attention is essential.

The information you leave on your answering machine or voicemail greeting should also be carefully considered. Avoid including personal details such as your full name, address, or work information. A simple message like, "Thank you for calling. Please leave a message, and I will return your call as soon as possible," is sufficient. Overly detailed greetings can unintentionally provide valuable information to scammers, making you a more attractive target. Instead, focus on the essentials – confirm that you received the message and will get back to them – without revealing sensitive personal data.

Remember, your greeting is publicly accessible to anyone who calls your number - whether their intentions are good or not. Keeping it brief and neutral is a simple yet effective way to improve your phone security. Similarly, avoid leaving voicemail messages that might unintentionally reveal confidential information. Remember, anything you say on voicemail is potentially accessible, so always exercise caution.

Another crucial aspect of mobile phone security is managing your apps. Only install apps from reputable sources, like official app stores, and take time to vet them carefully. Read user reviews and pay close attention to the permissions each app requests. If an app asks for excessive access - like to your contacts, location, or financial information - it could be a red flag. Malicious apps can steal personal information or install malware, creating vulnerabilities that scammers may exploit. Always be aware of what your apps can access and restrict permissions to only what's absolutely necessary to protect your privacy.

Regularly review the permissions granted to apps on your phone, and revoke access if any are no longer needed. By understanding and controlling the privileges your apps have, you take a significant step toward improving your phone's overall security and privacy. Additionally, promptly uninstall any apps you no longer use or suspect might be malicious - this helps eliminate unnecessary vulnerabilities from your system.

You can also disable or limit notifications from apps you don't use frequently. Excessive notifications can be distracting and increase your vulnerability to phishing attacks, where urgency can cloud your judgment.

Beyond app management, be mindful of your overall online behavior. Avoid clicking on unknown or suspicious links, even if they appear to be from someone you know. Scammers often use social engineering tactics to trick people into clicking on malicious links. If a link looks suspicious, don't click it. Instead, reach out to the sender directly to verify the message.

Similarly, be cautious when downloading attachments from unknown sources.

Malicious attachments can contain malware that compromises your phone's security. Always verify the sender's identity before opening or downloading anything. This simple precaution can significantly reduce your risk of exposure to malicious software.

And remember: if something seems too good to be true, it probably is. Stay aware of your surroundings and remain skeptical of unsolicited calls and communications. That kind of alertness is the bedrock of a strong, proactive security mindset.

In conclusion, protecting your phone and voicemail requires a multi-faceted approach. Combining strong technical security measures - like enabling call screening, blocking numbers, and keeping software updated - with smart behavioral practices, such as maintaining strong passwords and avoiding the disclosure of personal information, forms a robust defense against vishing attacks.

By actively managing your phone's settings, being vigilant with your apps, and remaining skeptical of unsolicited communications, you greatly reduce your vulnerability and strengthen your overall digital security. The combination of technical and behavioral safeguards creates a comprehensive strategy to protect you in today's complex digital landscape.

Remember: proactive security is far more effective - and far less costly - than reacting to a successful vishing attack.

Chapter 13: Call Authentication and Verification Methods

Building on our previous discussion about securing your phone and voicemail, we now turn our attention to the critical methods used to authenticate and verify incoming calls. Reliably identifying the true source of a phone call is paramount in combating vishing attacks, as many scams rely on deceiving you about the caller's identity. Although sophisticated spoofing techniques make this challenging, a mix of technological advancements and proactive steps can greatly improve your ability to stop legitimate callers and avoid falling victim to fraud.

One of the most fundamental tools in call authentication is Caller ID. While not foolproof, Caller ID shows the telephone number of the incoming call, letting you quickly assess whether the number looks familiar or suspicious. However, Caller ID is vulnerable to spoofing—where scammers manipulate the displayed number to appear legitimate. This technique is commonly used by many vishing perpetrators, who might show a number resembling your bank's customer service line or a government agency. This creates a false sense of urgency and legitimacy, encouraging you to engage with the call.

Therefore, relying solely on Caller ID as verification is inherently risky. Instead, it should be seen as one piece of the puzzle - a first-level screening tool that flags potentially suspicious calls. An unfamiliar or unusual number should trigger further investigation before you engage with the caller. Remember, a legitimate-looking number doesn't automatically guarantee authenticity.

Fortunately, advancements in caller ID technology are continually improving its ability to detect spoofed numbers. Many modern phone systems and telecommunications providers use sophisticated algorithms to analyze call patterns and identify potential spoofing attempts. These systems often rely on community-based reporting, where users flag suspicious calls, helping the algorithms learn and adapt to improve accuracy over time. Frequently, these systems will flag calls as "potential spam" or "likely scam" right on your caller ID display.

However, even with advanced caller ID technology, some uncertainty remains. While these systems greatly improve your ability to filter out many fraudulent calls, they aren't infallible. Always remain vigilant and take additional verification steps before sharing any sensitive information.

Beyond relying on technological solutions, proactive methods of verifying caller identity are essential. If you receive a call requesting personal information or demanding immediate action, never hesitate to take independent verification steps. One of the most effective methods is to hang up and contact the organization directly using a known, verified number - such as the one found on their official website or a business card. This allows you to independently confirm whether the original call was legitimate and whether the organization is truly requesting the information. When contacting an organization directly, be mindful of how you obtain the verification number – make sure it's from a trusted source.

Don't rely on the information provided by the original caller, and avoid using internet search engines to look up phone numbers, as spoofed websites can appear in search results. Instead, always use known, trustworthy resources to find the contact information you need. This cautious approach helps prevent scammers from directing you to their fraudulent websites or fake phone numbers.

In addition to contacting the organization directly, you can use several other verification methods. Cross-referencing information online can help confirm the legitimacy of a caller. Look for official announcements or press releases related to the issue in question. If a government agency claims to be contacting you, check whether the claim aligns with current policies or news reports. A quick search can often expose fraudulent claims and prevent you from sharing sensitive information with malicious actors.

Another important aspect of call verification is paying attention to the caller's communication style and tone. Legitimate organizations typically don't use high-pressure tactics or threatening language. Requests for immediate action - especially those involving sensitive financial or personal information - should always raise suspicion. Reputable organizations will give you time to verify their request through independent means and won't rush or pressure you into making quick decisions.

Furthermore, always be cautious of calls requesting remote access to your computer or other devices. This is a common tactic used by scammers to gain access to your systems and steal your data. Legitimate technical support personnel rarely ask for remote access and will likely be able to assist you without requiring such measures.

In addition to these methods, several services and applications can assist in verifying caller identity. Some providers offer reverse phone lookup services that provide additional information about a number, such as its registration details and any potential association with fraudulent activities. However, the accuracy and reliability of these services vary, so it's always best to corroborate any information obtained from these services with other sources. These services can provide valuable insights, but they should never be the sole basis for verifying a caller's identity.

The evolution of communication technologies has also brought forth new authentication methods. Many organizations now integrate multi-factor authentication (MFA) into their call systems. This often involves a second verification step, such as a one-time code sent via SMS or email, to confirm the identity of the caller before revealing sensitive information. The use of MFA greatly reduces the likelihood of successful vishing attacks, as it requires the scammer to gain access to more than just a phone number.

In conclusion, authenticating and verifying the identity of callers requires a multi-layered approach. While caller ID technology and its enhancements provide a valuable first line of defense, relying solely on technological solutions is insufficient. Proactive measures - including independent verification through direct contact with organizations and careful cross-referencing of information - are essential. By combining these technologies and practices, you significantly reduce your vulnerability to vishing attacks and enhance your overall digital security.

Remaining vigilant, skeptical, and proactive is the key to effectively combating these increasingly sophisticated threats. Genuine organizations will understand and appreciate your need to verify their identity before sharing any sensitive information. This caution isn't just a security measure - it's a demonstration of responsible digital citizenship. The combination of technological advancements and responsible behavior ultimately forms the strongest defense against vishing attacks.

Case Studies: Real-World Examples of Vishing Attacks

Case studies illuminate the insidious nature of vishing attacks and underscore the critical need for vigilance. Let's examine several real-world examples to better understand the diverse tactics employed by scammers - and the devastating consequences for their victims.

One frequently reported vishing tactic involves impersonating a financial institution. Scammers often call individuals, claiming to be from their bank's fraud department or a similar entity. They express concern about suspicious activity on the victim's account, creating a sense of urgency and fear. The scammer then manipulates the victim into revealing sensitive information - such as account numbers, PINs, online banking credentials, or Social Security numbers - under the guise of verifying account details or preventing fraudulent transactions.

In one documented case, a retiree received a call from someone claiming to be from her bank. Using a sophisticated voice-spoofing technique to mimic the genuine sound of a bank representative, the caller expressed concern about a series of unauthorized withdrawals from her savings account. Panicked, the retiree provided her account details and the one-time password

(OTP) she had received via text message, believing she was protecting her funds. Within minutes, the scammer transferred a significant portion of her life savings. The emotional distress experienced by the victim, coupled with the substantial financial loss, highlights the devastating impact of such attacks. This case illustrates how sophisticated voice-spoofing technology can make it incredibly difficult to distinguish between a genuine call and a scam.

Another common vishing tactic involves targeting individuals with tax-related scams. Scammers may impersonate representatives from the Internal Revenue Service (IRS), threatening victims with legal action or even imprisonment if they don't immediately pay an alleged - often inflated - tax bill. They use intimidating language, urgency, and details obtained through data breaches or other sources to create a sense of authenticity. Victims are frequently instructed to pay the false tax debt using prepaid debit cards or wire transfers, methods that make the funds extremely difficult to trace or recover.

One such case involved a small business owner who received a call from someone claiming to be an IRS agent. The caller accused the business owner of tax evasion and threatened legal action if a significant sum wasn't immediately paid. The caller provided a convincing amount of seemingly accurate personal and business information, including the business owner's address and tax ID number, which bolstered the scam's legitimacy. Fearing legal consequences, the business owner paid the fraudulent tax bill via wire transfer, only to realize it was a scam after the money was gone. This case reveals how readily available personal information can be weaponized by scammers to build credibility and heighten the sense of urgency among victims.

Vishing attacks are not limited to financial institutions and government agencies. Scammers increasingly target victims through other channels, such as fake technical support calls. They might call individuals claiming to be from a technology company, such as Microsoft or Apple, and report issues with the victim's computer or mobile device. The scammer then uses deceptive tactics to gain remote access to the victim's device, allowing them to steal data, install malware, or demand payment for bogus services.

One instance involved a college student who received a call from someone claiming to be a Microsoft technician. The caller stated that the student's computer had been infected with malware and offered to remotely assist in removing the threat. Believing the caller to be legitimate, the student granted remote access to their computer. The scammer then installed a remote access tool, stole personal data, and demanded a substantial payment for their services.

This case illustrates how scammers leverage technical expertise to manipulate victims into granting access to their systems, enabling further malicious activity. The use of remote access tools makes the scam more effective and harder to trace.

The consequences of vishing attacks extend beyond immediate financial losses. Victims often suffer significant emotional distress, including feelings of shame, anger, and violation. The betrayal of trust and sense of vulnerability can leave lasting psychological effects. Additionally, the fallout may impact on credit scores, insurance rates, and overall financial stability.

The cases described above represent just a small fraction of the countless vishing attacks occurring worldwide. As voice-spoofing technology evolves and scammers become increasingly sophisticated, the need for heightened awareness and proactive security measures grows more urgent. These attacks expose the vulnerabilities in our reliance on phone communication and highlight the importance of verifying information through trusted, independent channels.

To further demonstrate the wide reach of vishing attacks, let's explore scenarios that target different demographics:

Elderly individuals: Often targeted due to their perceived vulnerability and trust in authority figures, elderly individuals are frequent victims of vishing scams. Scammers typically pose as representatives of government agencies or financial institutions, exploiting the victim's unfamiliarity with newer technologies and a natural inclination to trust a convincing voice on the phone.

Small business owners: These individuals are frequently targeted with fake tax-related scams or calls demanding immediate payment for fraudulent invoices. The pressure to stay on top of financial obligations can prompt small business owners to act quickly, sometimes without taking the time to verify the authenticity of the request.

Students: Students may be especially susceptible to technical support scams, as they often lack the experience and technical know-how to recognize suspicious phone calls or emails. Scammers exploit their unfamiliarity with cybersecurity practices, making them prime targets for deceitful schemes.

These varied examples demonstrate the indiscriminate nature of vishing attacks, which impact a broad cross-section of society. In every case, the underlying tactic is the same: manipulating trust and creating a sense of urgency to extract sensitive information or financial gain.

Beyond these specific examples, it's important to recognize the rapidly evolving landscape of vishing techniques. Scammers continually adapt their methods, leveraging new technologies and exploiting emerging vulnerabilities. One major game-changer is the rise of artificial intelligence (AI), which now enables far more convincing voice impersonations and automated call systems. AI-powered tools can create realistic voice clones, making it increasingly difficult for victims to tell the difference between a legitimate call and a scam. This evolution highlights the urgent need for ongoing education and heightened awareness as these threats continue to advance.

In conclusion, understanding the real-world consequences of vishing attacks is crucial. The case studies highlighted here reveal the devastating financial and emotional toll these scams impose on individuals and organizations alike. By dissecting the tactics used and the vulnerabilities exploited, we gain a clearer appreciation for the need to stay vigilant, skeptical, and proactive in our defenses.

The next chapter will explore practical steps individuals can take to reduce their risk and enhance their overall digital security - empowering everyone to navigate today's complex communication landscape with confidence and safety.

Chapter 14: Understanding Smishing Tactics and Techniques

Smishing - a clever mashup of SMS and phishing - exploits the everyday reach of text messaging to trick people into handing over sensitive information or triggering malicious actions. Unlike phishing emails, which can often be spotted easily through email headers and sender verification, smishing attacks exploit the perceived immediacy and personal nature of text messages. The attacker's goal remains consistent across all forms of phishing: to gain access to your personal data, financial accounts, or install malware on your device. This section will dissect the tactics and techniques make smishing messages convincing and explore the psychological underpinnings of these attacks.

One of the most common tactics used in smishing is creating a sense of urgency. Messages often use phrases like "Your account has been compromised," "Urgent action required," or "Limited time offer," designed to pressure the recipient into quick, unthinking responses. This urgency bypasses rational thought, pushing victims to click malicious links or reveal sensitive information. For example, a message might claim a package delivery is pending and requires immediate confirmation of delivery address and credit card information through a provided link.

Another technique is personalization. Smishing attacks often use seemingly personalized greetings or details, such as the recipient's name or partial address, to build trust and credibility. This approach makes the message appear legitimate and less likely to be perceived as a scam. This information is often gathered from data breaches, social media profiles, or publicly accessible databases. The message might start with, "Hello, John," followed by a seemingly legitimate request, leading to a higher chance of the user clicking on the link or providing personal information.

The use of sophisticated spoofing techniques is also prevalent in smishing. Attackers can disguise the sender's phone number to appear as though the message is from a trusted source, such as a bank, a mobile carrier, or a government agency. This technique, known as caller ID spoofing, increases the likelihood that the recipient will trust the message's authenticity. For example, a message might appear to be from your bank, warning of suspicious activity and providing a link to verify account details. The similarity of the sender's number to the actual bank's registered number can easily trick someone into believing the message is legitimate.

Smishing messages often contain links to malicious websites. These websites mimic legitimate ones, such as online banking portals or e-commerce platforms, to trick users into entering their credentials or financial information. The URL might look very similar to a legitimate site but differ slightly, or it might be shortened using services like bit.ly, making it harder to determine its true nature. When the user clicks the link, they are redirected to a phishing website designed to steal their data. Some of these sites even display security certificates to boost their credibility.

Another prevalent tactic is the use of scare tactics. Messages may threaten the recipient with legal action, account suspension, or even arrest if they fail to take immediate action. This creates a sense of fear and panic, impairing rational decision-making and increasing the likelihood of compliance. A typical example would be a message stating, "Your account will be suspended unless you update your details within 24 hours by following this link [malicious link]." The urgency and threat of consequences pressure the user to act rashly without verifying the source.

The psychology behind smishing is crucial to understanding its effectiveness. These attacks exploit several human vulnerabilities: reliance on convenience, trust in authority figures, and a tendency to avoid conflict or confrontation. People are often more likely to respond quickly to a text message than a lengthy email, especially if it appears to come from a trusted source. The message's concise format and the immediacy of the SMS medium minimize the likelihood of critical thinking or seeking further verification. This inherent trust, combined with pressure to respond quickly, makes these attacks remarkably successful.

Consider these examples of smishing messages to illustrate the diverse techniques employed:

Example 1: The Urgent Delivery Scam:

"Your package from Amazon is delayed due to an incorrect address. Please update your details here: [malicious link]"

This message leverages urgency and the familiarity of online shopping to trick recipients.

Example 2: The Bank Security Alert:

"Your account has been compromised. Please verify your details immediately: [malicious link]. Your reference number is: [real or fabricated number]"

This approach uses social engineering to trick users into believing their security is at risk, leading to compliance.

Example 3: The IRS Impersonation:

"Your tax return is flagged for review. Please follow the link to update your information: [malicious link]. Failure to comply will result in penalties"

This message leverages the power of authority and the fear of legal consequences to coerce a reaction.

Example 4: The Tech Support Scam:

"Your phone is infected with malware! Please click here to fix it: [malicious link]"

This plays on the fear of technological issues and the urgency to resolve them quickly.

These examples highlight the various angles scammers use to bypass users' security awareness. Analyzing these examples, a critical reader may recognize patterns such as the use of urgency, authority, or fear - all aimed at exploiting the recipient's vulnerabilities.

To further enhance the effectiveness of their campaigns, smishing attackers often employ automated systems to send out mass messages. This significantly increases the reach of the campaign and the potential number of victims.

These systems can also personalize messages at scale, making them appear more targeted and legitimate.

Detecting smishing attempts requires a blend of critical thinking and awareness. Always approach unexpected messages with skepticism, especially those requesting personal information or directing you to unfamiliar websites. Avoid clicking on links in unsolicited messages, and verify the sender's identity through independent, trusted sources before sharing any sensitive data. Pay attention to the sender's number—even slight deviations from legitimate ones can indicate a scam. Watch for spelling and grammatical errors, which are common signs of fraudulent messages. If a message seems suspicious, reach out to the organization directly using a verified communication channel to confirm the message's authenticity.

In conclusion, understanding the tactics and techniques employed in smishing attacks is essential for protecting oneself from these increasingly sophisticated scams. By recognizing the psychological manipulation involved and the common traits of these messages, individuals can significantly reduce their vulnerability and avoid falling victim to such malicious schemes.

The next section will explore practical steps anyone can take to strengthen their digital security and mitigate the risks associated with smishing and related attacks.

Chapter 15: Identifying Malicious SMS Messages

Identifying a malicious SMS message requires a keen eye and a healthy dose of skepticism. While scammers constantly evolve their tactics, certain red flags consistently appear in fraudulent texts. Learning to recognize these indicators is your first line of defense against smishing attacks.

One of the most obvious, yet often overlooked, clues is the presence of spelling and grammatical errors. Legitimate organizations - especially banks, government agencies, and reputable companies - invest in professional communication.

Their messages are carefully crafted and reviewed for accuracy. A text riddled with typos, awkward phrasing, or incorrect grammar is a major warning sign. For example, a message saying, "Ur account has been compromised!" immediately raises suspicion. The casual, informal tone and poor grammar are starkly different from the formal language typically used by financial institutions.

Beyond simple spelling errors, watch for inconsistencies in language and tone. Does the message abruptly shift from formal to informal language? Or stay overly formal, like it's trying too hard in a text? Such odd shifts often indicate a hastily crafted scam message. For example: "Dear Valued Customer, your account is in jeopardy. lol, just kidding, unless...? Click here: [malicious link]". The sudden flip from formal business language to casual slang is a glaring red flag.

Suspicious links are another major red flag in malicious SMS messages. Legitimate organizations rarely send links via text asking for sensitive information. If you get a text with a link, never click it directly. Instead, independently verify the sender's identity and the link's legitimacy through other means - like checking the organization's official website or calling customer support using a known phone number. Be especially wary of shortened URLs (like those using bit.ly or tinyurl.com) since they mask the true destination, making it harder to tell if the link is malicious. Hover your mouse over the link (if you're on a computer) to preview the actual URL before clicking – though keep in mind, this isn't a guarantee of safety. Legitimate organizations typically use their own domains in official communications.

Requests for personal information via SMS should always raise alarm bells. Legitimate businesses rarely ask for sensitive data like passwords, credit card numbers, Social Security numbers, or bank account details through text messages. If a message asks for this kind of information, it's almost certainly a scam. Even if the message appears to come from a trusted source, always double-check by contacting the organization through a verified channel—preferably using a phone number found on their official website, not the one provided in the text.

Threats are a common tactic used by smishing scammers. Messages may warn of immediate account suspension, legal action, or even arrest if you don't respond immediately. This sense of urgency is designed to short-circuit your critical thinking and pressure you into acting rashly.

While some legitimate communications might include warnings, they rarely involve explicit threats or ultimatums - especially when requesting personal information. Legitimate institutions focus on offering solutions, not making threats.

The sender's phone number can provide valuable clues. While spoofing techniques allow scammers to disguise their numbers, a careful look can still reveal inconsistencies. Watch for unusual area codes or numbers that don't match the claimed sender. For example, a message claiming to be from your bank in London might have a phone number from a completely different country. Likewise, numbers with too many digits or odd formatting can signal spoofing or fraud. Keep in mind that most banks today rely on official mobile apps rather than sending sensitive information via text.

Beyond these key indicators, pay attention to the overall context of the message. Does it make logical sense? Does the request match how you typically interact with the supposed sender? If something feels off or unusual, it's best to err on the side of caution. Think about how often you've communicated via text with the organization, and whether the message content aligns with past interactions.

Let's look at some real-world examples to illustrate these points.

Example 1: The "Urgent Payment" Scam:

"Your Netflix subscription is overdue. To avoid service interruption, pay $19.99 immediately at [malicious link]."

This message raises several red flags. The link is suspicious and could lead to a fake payment page designed to steal your credit card information.

Netflix typically sends email reminders about overdue payments - not SMS messages demanding immediate action.

Example 2: The "Package Delivery" Scam:

"Your package is delayed due to an incorrect address. Update your details at [malicious link] or your package will be returned."

While package delays do happen, it's unusual for a delivery service to request personal information via a shortened URL in a text message. Reputable delivery services provide tracking information accessible through their official websites, and usually communicate via email.

Example 3: The "Government Grant" Scam:

"You've been approved for a government grant of $5000! Claim your money now at [malicious link]."

Government grants are rarely, if ever, advertised through SMS messages. Scammers use messages like these to lure victims into phishing schemes. Legitimate government agencies communicate through official channels - not random, too-good-to-be-true text messages.

Example 4: The "Bank Security Alert" Scam:

"Security alert! Your account shows unusual activity. Verify your details here: [malicious link]. This is a secure link provided by [Bank Name]."

This is a classic smishing scam. While banks do send security alerts, they would typically use official banking apps, verified email addresses, or known phone numbers. They **never** ask for personal login credentials through unsecured channels like SMS.

In conclusion, spotting malicious SMS messages requires a proactive and critical mindset. By carefully examining the message for spelling errors, suspicious links, unusual requests for personal information, threats, and inconsistencies in the sender's identity, you can greatly reduce your risk of falling for a smishing attack. When in doubt, always verify the information through a known, legitimate channel – completely separate from the text - before taking any action. Your vigilance is your best defence against these increasingly sophisticated scams.

Chapter 16: Mobile Security Best Practices for Smishing Prevention

Securing your mobile device is paramount in the fight against smishing. Think of your phone as a digital wallet – it holds your financial information, personal details, and access to various online accounts. Protecting this device is as crucial as safeguarding your physical wallet. Fortunately, a few simple yet highly effective measures can significantly bolster your mobile security and make you a far less appealing target for smishing scams.

One of the most powerful tools at your disposal is two-factor authentication (2FA). It adds an extra layer of security to your online accounts by requiring not only your password but also a second form of verification, such as a code sent to your phone via SMS or a verification app. While it might seem like an extra step, 2FA dramatically reduces the risk of unauthorized access - even if a scammer manages to obtain your password. Enable it for all your important accounts, including email, banking apps, social media platforms, and online shopping accounts. However, be aware that even with 2FA, some smishing attacks may attempt to circumvent this security measure. Stay vigilant, and never click links sent via SMS.

Regularly updating your mobile operating system (OS) and apps is another crucial aspect of mobile security. Software updates often include security patches that address vulnerabilities scammers could exploit. Neglecting these updates leaves your device susceptible to attack. Make it a habit to install updates as soon as they become available. Most modern smartphones will notify you when updates are ready. For apps, check for updates in the app store regularly or enable automatic updates. This ensures you're always running the latest, most secure versions of both your OS and apps.

Downloading apps exclusively from official app stores is a critical step. While alternative app stores exist, these can be breeding grounds for malicious software. Stick to reputable sources like the Google Play Store for Android devices and the Apple App Store for iPhones and iPads.

Before installing any app, carefully read user reviews and check the app's permissions. If an app requests access to more information than it needs, that's a red flag. Only install apps you fully trust and actually need – this helps minimize your potential attack surface.

Caution when clicking links is vital. Never click links in unsolicited text messages. Legitimate organizations rarely send sensitive links through SMS. If you receive a message containing a link, don't click it. Instead, independently verify the message's legitimacy. Look up the organization's official contact information through a trusted source, such as their official website or a phone book, and contact them directly. This simple step can keep you from falling prey to fake websites designed to steal your information. Consider adding the phone numbers for your bank and other key organizations to your contacts. Never use numbers provided in untrusted SMS messages.

Avoid responding to unsolicited requests for personal information. Legitimate organizations will never ask for sensitive details like passwords, credit card numbers, Social Security numbers, or bank account information via SMS. If you receive such a request, it's almost certainly a scam. Never provide any personal information unless you've initiated contact with the organization yourself through a verified channel. Remember - reputable companies typically don't ask for sensitive data in text messages.

Be cautious of messages creating a sense of urgency. Scammers often try to pressure you into acting quickly by threatening immediate account suspension, legal action, or other dire consequences. This urgency is designed to bypass your critical thinking. Take your time to investigate before responding to any message using this tactic.

Consider using a password manager. Password managers are programs designed to generate and store strong, unique passwords for your various online accounts. This makes it much harder for attackers to gain access to your information, even if one account is compromised. A good password manager lets you to easily create and manage unique passwords for every account, preventing credential stuffing attacks - where attackers try using the same password across multiple websites. Most also offer 2FA, increasing your overall security.

Regularly review your phone's permissions. Check your settings to ensure apps only have the permissions they truly need. If you find an app with excessive permissions – especially to your contacts, location, or microphone - uninstall it immediately. This is crucial, as many malicious apps attempt to gain unauthorized access to your personal information.

Stay informed about current smishing scams by keeping up cybersecurity news and advisories. Awareness of latest tactics will help you quickly spot suspicious messages. Numerous reputable cybersecurity resources regularly share information on common scams.

Understand the limitations of security measures. No solution is foolproof. Even with all the precautions in place, there's always a small risk of falling victim to a scam. However, by following these mobile security best practices, you can greatly reduce your vulnerability to smishing attacks.

As stated in previous chapters, always use caution with public Wi-Fi networks. Public Wi-Fi is often unsecured, making your device more vulnerable to attacks. Avoid accessing sensitive information, such as banking apps or online shopping sites, while connected to these networks. Consider using a VPN for added security – it encrypts your data, making it much harder for attackers to intercept your information.

Keep your device software up-to-date - including your operating system, apps, and any security software. Regular updates contain critical security patches that fix vulnerabilities and help protect against malware.

Regularly back up your phone's data to a secure location, such as a cloud service or an external hard drive. This ensures you won't lose your important information if your device is lost, stolen, or compromised.

Be cautious of unsolicited calls and messages. Don't respond to calls or messages from unknown numbers, and never provide personal information to someone you don't recognize.

Report suspicious activity. If you believe you've been the victim of a smishing attack, report it to the appropriate authorities. This helps law enforcement track down scammers and prevent future attacks.

In summary, while technology constantly evolves and smishing tactics adapt, the core principles of mobile security remain the same: vigilance, skepticism, and proactive protection. By implementing these best practices, you're significantly strengthening your defenses against this pervasive threat and taking control of your digital safety. Remember - your proactive approach is your strongest weapon against smishing.

Chapter 17: Responding to Suspicious SMS Messages

The first rule of responding to a suspicious SMS message is: don't engage! Resist the urge to reply, even to express anger or disbelief. Responding – positively or negatively - confirms to the scammer that your number is active and potentially vulnerable. It's like feeding a troll: the more you interact, the more persistent they become. In this case, silence is your strongest weapon.

This inaction goes beyond simply not replying - it also means absolutely no clicking on any links included in the message. These links are almost always designed to lead you to a fake website mimicking a legitimate organization. The site may look authentic, complete with logos and design elements that closely resemble the real thing, but it's a carefully crafted trap. Clicking these links could result in malware being installed on your phone, the theft of your personal data, or redirection to phishing pages designed to steal your login credentials. Even if the link appears to go to a well-known website - like your bank's - never trust a link embedded in an unsolicited SMS.

Instead of clicking, verify the legitimacy of the message independently. Look up the official contact information for the purported sender—whether it's your bank, a delivery service, or other organization—using a trusted source like their official website or a physical phone book (yes, those still exist!). Then contact them directly using the number you found. Explain the text message you received and ask about its authenticity. A legitimate organization will be happy to confirm or deny the message's validity and guide you through any necessary actions.

Blocking the sender's number is another crucial step. This prevents future messages from that number from reaching your phone, effectively silencing the immediate threat. The method for blocking varies by mobile operating system. For Android users, it usually involves opening the messaging app, finding the conversation with the suspicious number, accessing message options, and selecting "Block." iOS users follow a similar process, though steps might vary depending on the messaging app used. Check your phone's manual or online resources for instructions specific to your device.

Blocking is an effective measure against repeat offenders, but it is no guarantee against future smishing attempts. Scammers often use different numbers or spoof legitimate ones to mask their identity. That's why staying vigilant and skeptical remains crucial, even after you block a number.

Reporting suspicious messages is vital in the fight against smishing. This helps law enforcement and cybersecurity agencies track scammers and take action. The reporting process varies by location and the nature of the scam. In many countries, you can report smishing attempts to your mobile carrier and local law enforcement. Some countries also have dedicated cybercrime reporting centers. Research your local resources to learn the best way to report.

Your mobile carrier can play a significant role in mitigating the impact of smishing. They have systems to flag and block malicious numbers, helping prevent widespread scams. By reporting suspicious messages to your carrier, you contribute to a larger effort to combat smishing and make the network safer for everyone.

Beyond these immediate responses, consider taking further precautions to enhance your overall mobile security. Regularly review your phone's security settings to ensure robust password protection, two-factor authentication where possible, and that all software updates are installed. Remember - a well-protected phone is much less likely to fall victim to smishing attempts.

If you suspect you've fallen prey to a smishing attempt and shared sensitive information - like banking details, Social Security number, or passwords - act swiftly. Contact your bank or relevant institutions immediately to report the incident and secure your accounts. Consider freezing your credit to prevent fraudulent activity as well.

It's also advisable to review your bank and credit card statements regularly for unauthorized transactions. Keep a close eye on even small amounts – as scammers frequently test the waters by doing a few small transactions before trying for larger amounts - early detection is key to minimizing potential financial losses.

The aftermath of a smishing attack can be unsettling, but proactive steps can lessen the impact. The key is to stay informed, act decisively, and remain vigilant. Remember, even experienced users can fall victim to well-crafted smishing attacks - but taking the right precautions significantly reduces your vulnerability.

Let's delve deeper into common smishing scenarios and how to respond effectively. Imagine receiving a text claiming to be from your bank, warning of suspicious activity on your account and directing you to a website to verify your details. This is a classic smishing tactic. Your immediate response should be to avoid engaging with the message. Don't click any links. Instead, find your bank's legitimate contact information - on your bank card or their official website - and call them directly to verify the message's authenticity. If the bank confirms no suspicious activity, you can safely disregard the smishing attempt. Be sure to report the message to both your bank and the authorities.

Another common scenario is a message posing as a delivery service, claiming you missed a delivery and asking for personal information to reschedule. Again, stay calm and verify the message's authenticity through independent channels before responding.

Do not provide any personal information. Instead, contact the delivery service directly using verified contact information from their website or receipt to confirm the delivery attempt. If no such delivery was attempted, you can safely assume it's a scam.

What about a message claiming to be from a government agency, warning of an outstanding tax payment or legal action? Scammers often use these messages to create a sense of urgency and pressure victims into acting quickly. Never provide sensitive information in response.

Instead, contact the relevant government agency directly through official channels to verify the message's authenticity. Their official websites usually have the contact details you need.

In each of these scenarios, maintaining a skeptical mindset and relying on independent verification is crucial. Remember, legitimate organizations rarely send sensitive requests or notifications via text message. Always verify information through trusted channels before taking any action.

Beyond individual responses to suspicious SMS messages, consider broader strategies to enhance your overall mobile security. Keep your mobile operating system and apps updated regularly to benefit from the latest security patches. Enable two-factor authentication (2FA) wherever possible to add an extra layer of protection to your online accounts. Be mindful of the permissions you grant apps, ensuring they only access what's necessary. Avoid clicking links from unknown sources or unsolicited messages.

Finally, educate yourself and stay informed about the latest smishing trends. Many reputable cybersecurity websites and organizations regularly share information and awareness campaigns about current scams. Staying informed improves your ability to identify and avoid these threats. Your vigilance, coupled with these proactive measures, is your best defense against smishing. Remember, even the smallest detail can alert you to a potentially harmful message. Take your time, be cautious, and stay safe.

Chapter 18: Case Studies – Real World Smishing Scams

Let's now examine specific instances of smishing attacks to understand their real-world impact and the diverse tactics used by scammers. These case studies highlight the creativity and persistence of cybercriminals, emphasizing the importance of constant vigilance and proactive security measures.

Case Study 1: The "Urgent Bank Alert" Scam

This widespread smishing campaign targets banking customers with messages claiming urgent action is required due to suspicious account activity. The message typically creates a sense of urgency and panic by using phrases like "Your account has been compromised" or "Immediate action required." It includes a hyperlink directing the recipient to a convincing imitation of the bank's website. This fake website is carefully designed to mimic the real one - matching layout, color scheme, and logos - making it difficult to detect the fraud. Once the victim enters their login credentials and other sensitive information, the scammers gain access to their accounts, often resulting in financial loss and identity theft.

This scam's effectiveness lies in its ability to exploit the victim's trust in their bank. The urgency compels quick action, often bypassing critical thinking. The convincing fake website reinforces the deception, successfully prompting many individuals to share their personal information. The consequences can range from minor financial losses to complete bank account depletion and long-term damage to one's credit history. This case study highlights the importance of independently verifying any communication that claims to be from a financial institution, never clicking on links in unsolicited messages, and contacting the bank directly through official channels if there's any suspicion of fraud.

Case Study 2: The "Package Delivery" Deception

This smishing tactic takes advantage of the widespread use of online shopping and delivery services. The message claims a failed delivery attempt and prompts the victim to click a link to reschedule or provide additional information. That link typically leads to a fake website designed to collect personal details, credit card numbers, or other sensitive data. This information is then used for identity theft, fraudulent transactions, or other malicious purposes.

The scam's success lies in its relatability and the illusion of convenience. With so many people regularly receiving packages, a message about a missed delivery seems entirely plausible. The urgency to receive the package, combined with a seemingly legitimate request for information, often overrides caution. The consequences can be serious, ranging from financial loss to identity theft and compromised personal data. This case emphasizes the importance of verifying delivery information independently, never providing personal information via SMS, and contacting the delivery service directly through its official website or the phone number provided in the original delivery confirmation.

Case Study 3: The "Government Impersonation" Fraud

Smishing attacks often impersonate government agencies, such as the IRS or Social Security Administration. These messages typically threaten legal action, fines, or suspension of services unless the recipient takes immediate action - usually by clicking a link or providing sensitive information. The link often leads to a fake website designed to collect personal data or install malware on the victim's phone. The perceived authority and fear associated with government agencies make this scam incredibly effective.

This type of smishing attack exploits the fear of legal consequences and the public's trust in official government institutions. The message's threatening tone creates a false sense of urgency that can override critical thinking and compel victims to act without verifying the messages. The consequences can be severe, leading to financial loss, identity theft, and legal issues. It's essential never to provide personal information or click on links in unsolicited messages claiming to be from a government agency. Always verify the communication by contacting the agency directly through official, trusted channels.

Case Study 4: The "Lottery Win" or "Prize Notification" Hoax

This type of smishing scam promises a significant prize, lottery win, or unexpected reward. Victims are often instructed to click a link to claim their prize or provide their personal information to process the winnings. The link usually leads to a fake website designed to collect personal data or install malware. The allure of a substantial reward and the excitement of a possible win can make individuals especially vulnerable to this kind of deception.

This scam capitalizes on human desire and the possibility of unexpected gain. The excitement and potential financial reward often cloud judgment, making individuals more susceptible to clicking links and providing personal information without sufficient scrutiny. The consequences can include financial loss, malware infection, or identity theft. Remember: legitimate organizations rarely announce major prizes or wins via text messages. Any such communication should be treated with extreme caution and independently verified.

Case Study 5: The "Account Update" Request

Many smishing campaigns target online accounts, such as social media platforms, email providers, or online retail accounts. The messages often claim there is a need to update account information, verify details, or reset a password. Victims are asked to click a link that leads to a fake login page, where they are tricked into entering their credentials. The scammers then gain access to the accounts, potentially causing financial loss, data theft, or reputational harm.

This scam relies on the frequency of legitimate account updates and password resets. It's designed to seem routine and familiar, easily blending in with real communications.

This familiarity increases the likelihood that recipients will overlook red flags and click the provided link. The consequences can range from account takeover to data breaches and financial loss. Always verify any request to update account information through the official website or app of the service provider. Never click links from unsolicited messages requesting personal information or login credentials.

Analysis and Prevention

These case studies demonstrate the diverse tactics used in smishing attacks and their potential to cause significant harm. The common threads among these examples are the creation of urgency, the use of deception, and the exploitation of trust.

Preventing smishing attacks requires a multifaceted approach:

Education: Raising awareness about smishing techniques is crucial. Understanding common tactics and red flags empowers individuals to recognize and respond to suspicious messages.

Verification: Always independently verify any information received through SMS, especially messages requesting personal data or urgent action. Contact the organization directly using official contact information found on their website or another trusted source.

Caution: Exercise caution when clicking links in SMS messages. Avoid clicking on any links from unknown senders or messages that seem suspicious.

Security Software: Install and regularly update security software on your mobile device to help protect against malware.

Two-Factor Authentication (2FA): Enable 2FA on all important online accounts to add an extra layer of security.

Reporting: Report suspicious SMS messages to your mobile carrier and appropriate authorities. Doing so aids in tracking down scammers and preventing future attacks.

By understanding the techniques used in real-world smishing scams and implementing effective preventive measures, individuals can significantly reduce their vulnerability to these pervasive threats. Remember, vigilance and skepticism are your strongest defenses in the ever-evolving world of cybercrime. The cost of complacency can be high - proactive measures are the key to staying safe in the digital landscape.

Chapter 19: Spear Phishing and Whaling Attacks

Spearphishing and whaling are both targeted forms of phishing, but they differ primarily in the profile of their victims and the scale of their impact. Spearphishing involves personalized phishing attacks targeting specific individuals within an organization, often utilizing tailored information to enhance credibility and deceive recipients into divulging sensitive data or credentials. In contrast, whaling targets high-ranking executives or decision-makers—such as CEOs, CFOs, or board members—who have access to more valuable information and financial assets. Whaling attacks often use more sophisticated tactics and professional-looking communications to exploit the authority and influence of their targets, potentially resulting in more significant financial or reputational damage.

Spearphishing and whaling attacks represent a significant escalation in phishing techniques. Unlike generic phishing campaigns that cast a wide net, these attacks are meticulously targeted, leveraging extensive reconnaissance to craft highly personalized messages aimed at deceiving specific individuals or organizations. This level of personalization dramatically increases the likelihood of success, as the messages appear genuine and trustworthy, bypassing the skepticism typically triggered by generic phishing emails.

The foundation of spear phishing and whaling lies in meticulous intelligence gathering. Attackers spend considerable time researching their targets, often using publicly available information like social media profiles, company websites, and news articles. They piece together details about the target's personal life, professional roles, and relationships to craft a highly convincing narrative within the phishing email or message. This careful research lets them tailor the attack to the individual's interests, responsibilities, and even current projects. For example, a spear phishing attempt targeting a finance executive might involve a fake invoice tied to a recent acquisition or a seemingly legitimate email discussing an important upcoming investment opportunity. The level of detail and personalization makes these attacks incredibly difficult to detect.

Whaling attacks represent the most sophisticated and high-value form of spear phishing. They specifically target high-profile individuals within an organization such as CEOs, CFOs, or other senior executives who have access to significant financial resources, sensitive data, or critical business information. The potential payoff for successful whaling attacks is substantially higher, motivating attackers to invest more time and resources into their planning and execution. These attacks often involve a multi-stage approach, utilizing various techniques to build trust and establish credibility before requesting the target to perform an action, such as transferring funds or revealing sensitive credentials. The attackers may employ techniques like sending seemingly legitimate business proposals, impersonating trusted colleagues or business partners, or creating a sense of urgency to pressure the target into acting quickly without careful consideration.

A key element of both spear phishing and whaling is the creation of a believable pretext. This involves carefully crafting a story or scenario that justifies the attacker's request for information or action. This pretext may involve a fictitious business opportunity, a seemingly urgent security alert, or a request for sensitive information under the guise of an official company policy or legal requirement. The attacker's goal is to create a sense of urgency and legitimacy, overwhelming the target's natural skepticism and prompting them to bypass standard security protocols. The more intricate and convincing the pretext, the higher the chances of success.

The technical aspects of these advanced phishing attacks are just as sophisticated. Attackers often use advanced techniques like email spoofing - forging the sender's email address to make the message appear to come from a trusted source. This makes it extremely hard to spot the email as fraudulent, even for experienced users. They may also deliver malware through clever methods, such as embedding malicious links or attachments that automatically download and install malware onto the victim's computer once clicked. This malware can then steal sensitive data, take remote control the victim's computer, or gain access to the organization's network.

Furthermore, attackers often use social engineering techniques to manipulate the target's emotions and perceptions. These might involve creating a sense of urgency, appealing to the target's sense of responsibility, or exploiting their trust in authority figures. For example, a whaling attack might mimic the style and tone of the CEO's previous messages, making the email seem perfectly authentic and increasing the likelihood of the target complying with the attacker's request. The attacker's skill at psychological manipulation is a key factor in the success of these attacks.

The success rate of spear phishing and whaling attacks is significantly higher than generic phishing campaigns. That's because they're highly targeted and personalized, using the attacker's detailed knowledge of the target's vulnerabilities and context. As a result, these attacks can result in severe consequences for both individuals and organizations - including financial losses, data breaches, reputational damage, and operational disruptions. Compromised credentials can open the door to further attacks on those accounts, causing cascading damage to both the individual and the organization.

Preventing spear phishing and whaling attacks requires a multi-layered approach that involves both technical and human factors. On the technical side, robust email security solutions with advanced anti-spoofing and malware detection capabilities are essential. Organizations should also implement strong authentication mechanisms, such as multi-factor authentication (MFA), to make it significantly harder for attackers to gain unauthorized access to accounts - even if they obtain credentials through phishing. Regular security awareness training for employees is also critical. This training should educate staff on the tactics used in spear phishing and whaling attacks, stressing the importance of verifying the authenticity of communications before taking action. Employees should be encouraged to report suspicious emails immediately. Training simulations can help demonstrate the subtle complexities of these attacks and prepare staff to identify and respond effectively.

A crucial element of prevention involves fostering a culture of security awareness within the organization. This culture should encourage employees to question the authenticity of communications - especially those containing sensitive information or urgent requests. It requires a shift in mindset, promoting critical thinking and skepticism over immediate compliance. Regular employee education and training must work hand-in-hand with technological security measures to create a comprehensive approach to preventing these costly and impactful attacks.

Furthermore, organizations should implement robust incident response plans to mitigate the damage from successful phishing attacks. These plans should clearly outline the steps for identifying, containing, and recovering from a security incident, minimizing the potential impact on the organization's operations and reputation. They should also include procedures for promptly reporting incidents to relevant authorities and affected parties.

In summary, spear phishing and whaling attacks represent a sophisticated and evolving threat to both individuals and organizations. Their effectiveness lies in their personalized nature and reliance on meticulous intelligence gathering and social engineering. Effective prevention demands a robust, layered security approach that includes technical safeguards, employee training, and a culture of security awareness - emphasizing constant vigilance and a proactive stance on cybersecurity. The consequences of successful attacks are severe, making investment in preventive measures a critical necessity. The cost of inaction far outweighs the cost of comprehensive cybersecurity protection.

Chapter 20: The Role of Malware in Phishing Attacks

The sophistication of modern phishing attacks goes far beyond cleverly crafted emails. A critical element of many successful campaigns is the strategic deployment of malware, which acts as an insidious backdoor, giving attackers persistent access to victim systems and enabling the exfiltration of sensitive data. Understanding the role of malware in these attacks is crucial to mounting an effective defense. This isn't just about clicking a malicious link - it's about recognizing the multifaceted ways attackers use malware to achieve their goals, turning a seemingly harmless interaction into a serious security breach.

One of the most common forms of malware used in phishing attacks is the keylogger. These insidious programs secretly record every keystroke made on the infected device. This means that attackers can gain access not only to passwords and credit card details, but also to any sensitive information entered into online forms, emails, or messaging apps. The information captured by keyloggers isn't limited to credentials - it can include personal communications, financial transactions, and even intellectual property, depending on the victim's online activities.

The keylogger's silent operation makes detection challenging, as victims are often completely unaware their activity is being monitored. Attackers may use the captured information immediately for malicious purposes or collect it over time to launch a larger attack, such as identity theft or corporate espionage. The longer the keylogger goes undetected, the greater the potential damage.

Ransomware presents a more aggressive and immediate threat. Unlike keyloggers, which operate quietly in the background, ransomware encrypts the victim's files, rendering them inaccessible until a ransom is paid. Phishing emails often contain malicious attachments or links that trigger a ransomware download. Once executed, the ransomware quickly locks down the system and displays a message demanding payment - typically in cryptocurrency - to store access to the data.

The pressure to pay the ransom stems not only from the loss of data but also from the implied threat of data leakage or further malicious activity. The ransom amount can vary widely, depending on the perceived value of the victim's data and the sophistication of the ransomware. Critically, paying the ransom offers no guarantee of data recovery - many ransomware operators simply take the payment without providing a decryption key. Furthermore, paying the ransom can unintentionally fund further criminal activity and encourage similar attacks in the future.

Trojan horses represent another significant threat vector. These malicious programs disguise themselves as legitimate software or files, often delivered through seemingly harmless attachments or links embedded in phishing emails.

Once the victim executes the Trojan, it can grant attackers remote access to the system, allowing them to steal data, install additional malware, and control the victim's actions.

Trojans can be highly versatile, operating quietly in the background to carry out a range of malicious functions - from simple data theft to more complex actions like manipulating system settings or launching distributed denial-of-service (DDoS) attacks. They're often used as a foothold for more extensive attacks, allowing attackers to move beyond the initially compromised device and deeper into the victim's network. The silent nature of Trojans and their ability to blend into the system makes them especially dangerous.

The delivery methods for these malware variants are often cleverly disguised. Malicious links might look harmless, pointing to what seem like legitimate websites. The URLs are often carefully crafted to mimic authentic website addresses, making it difficult even for experienced users to spot the fraudulent links. Attackers also use URL shorteners to further hide the real destination, concealing the true nature of the link. Malicious attachments often disguise themselves as everyday files like documents, spreadsheets, or images - tempting users to open and execute them.

These attachments can contain macros that execute malicious code or be specially crafted to exploit vulnerabilities in the victim's software. Drive-by downloads are another common method, where malware installs itself automatically without the victim's consent - often by exploiting weaknesses in the browser or operating system. These attacks can happen just by visiting a compromised website, showing how vulnerable users are even without clicking malicious links or opening attachments.

Protecting against malware infections requires a multi-layered approach. The first line of defense is strong email security - spam filters, antivirus software, and powerful anti-phishing filters that identify and block malicious emails before they even reach the user's inbox.

Educating users about phishing tactics and the dangers of opening suspicious emails or attachments is equally crucial. Security awareness training should go beyond just raising awareness - it needs to equip users with the knowledge and tools to spot and report phishing attempts, understand malware risks, and recognize the many ways malware can be delivered. This kind of training is especially important in organizations, where the financial and reputational damage from a successful phishing attack can be much more severe.

Beyond email security, robust endpoint protection is essential. This includes up-to-date antivirus and anti-malware software, along with firewalls and intrusion detection systems to monitor network traffic for suspicious activity. Regular software updates are critical to patch vulnerabilities that attackers exploit to deliver malware.

Software vulnerabilities are often exploited by malicious actors to gain system access, so keeping all software updated is crucial in preventing exploits.

Using multi-factor authentication (MFA) on all critical online accounts significantly reduces the damage caused by compromised credentials - even if malware steals passwords. MFA adds an additional layer of security by requiring a second form of authentication, often a code sent to a mobile device, to verify the user's identity. This is a crucial step in limiting the fallout, even when phishing attacks succeed in capturing passwords.

Furthermore, regularly backing up important data is essential to reduce the impact of ransomware attacks. Backups allow data to be restored even if it's encrypted by ransomware, eliminating the need to pay a ransom and minimizing disruption. Storing backups offline or in a physically secure location adds an extra layer of protection against attackers trying to access or destroy them. Implementing data loss prevention (DLP) tools can also help organizations monitor and prevent sensitive data from leaving the network. These tools analyze network traffic and block suspicious activity in real time.

In conclusion, malware plays a pivotal role in the success of many modern phishing attacks. Understanding the types of malwares used, their delivery methods, and the potential impact on victims is essential for effective prevention. The strongest defense is a multi-layered approach that combines robust technical safeguards with comprehensive user education and awareness training.

The consequences of a successful malware infection can be devastating, extending far beyond the initial breach and affecting individuals and organizations for extended periods. Proactive security measures, paired with continuous vigilance, are key to mitigating the ever-evolving threats posed by malware in phishing campaigns. Ultimately, investing in strong security systems and user education is far less costly than managing the aftermath of a successful attack - financial losses, reputational damage, and operational disruptions that could take months or even years to recover from.

Chapter 21: Phishing Kits and Attack Infrastructure

The preceding discussion highlighted the critical role of malware in modern phishing attacks. However, the success of these campaigns relies not only on the malicious software used but also on the sophisticated tools and infrastructure that support their execution. This section explores the technical foundations of advanced phishing attacks, focusing on the readily available tools that make these campaigns easier to launch, as well as the complex infrastructure attackers use to remain anonymous and effective.

One of the most significant developments in the phishing landscape is the rise of phishing kits. These pre-built packages - often sold on dark web marketplaces - equip attackers with all the components needed to launch a phishing campaign with minimal technical skill. Think of them as plug-and-play attack tools, streamlining everything from crafting convincing phishing emails to collecting stolen credentials.

Phishing kits typically include website templates that mimic legitimate services like banks, email providers, or social media platforms, often using sophisticated visual design to fool unsuspecting victims. These templates are highly customizable, allowing attackers to tailor their messages to specific audiences or campaigns.

The ease of use provided by these kits is a major concern. Even individuals with limited technical skills can launch sophisticated phishing attacks, significantly lowering the barrier to entry for cybercriminals. This accessibility leads to a surge in the volume and frequency of phishing attempts, straining the resources of security professionals and increasing the chances of successful attacks.

Many kits also come equipped with features designed to conceal the attacker's true identity and evade detection. These can include obfuscated code, encrypted communication channels, and techniques that redirect traffic through multiple servers, making it difficult to trace the attack back to its source.

Phishing kits typically contain a comprehensive set of components. They often include ready-made phishing email templates - complete with subject lines and body text - crafted to lure victims into clicking malicious links or opening attachments. These templates are frequently highly personalized, incorporating seemingly legitimate details like the victim's name or a recent transaction to increase credibility.

In addition, phishing kits often provide pre-built phishing websites, designed to mimic legitimate login pages or forms. These sites are meticulously crafted to look authentic, complete with logos, branding, and even security certificates to further enhance their legitimacy. The functionality of these sites extends beyond just collecting credentials; they often include capabilities to record keystrokes, capture screenshots, and install malware on the victim's machine. Phishing kits can even include instructions on how to deploy and manage the attack, making the entire process remarkably easy for even the most technically inept attacker.

Beyond the kits themselves, the infrastructure supporting these attacks is equally critical. Attackers rely on a network of compromised servers, often located across multiple jurisdictions, to host their phishing websites and manage their operations. These servers act as command-and-control centers, relaying instructions to infected devices and collecting stolen data. The use of multiple servers scattered geographically makes it challenging for law enforcement and security researchers to track down the perpetrators. The servers themselves may be compromised through various methods, including vulnerabilities in web applications, weak passwords, or brute-force attacks. Once compromised, these servers are often used for a multitude of malicious activities, demonstrating the significant threat they pose to the broader internet ecosystem.

The use of botnets further amplifies the scale and reach of phishing attacks. A botnet is a network of compromised computers, or "bots," remotely controlled by attackers. These bots are often used to send out massive numbers of phishing emails, overwhelm security systems, and distribute malware.

The sheer scale of a botnet attack makes it incredibly difficult to filter out all malicious emails, increasing the likelihood that some phishing messages will reach their intended targets. The decentralized nature of a botnet also makes it harder to identify and neutralize the attackers, allowing them to maintain persistent and highly effective campaigns.

To further obscure their tracks, attackers often use anonymization services. These mask the attacker's IP address and other identifying information, making it nearly impossible to trace the attacks origin. Virtual Private Networks (VPNs), proxies, and Tor networks are common tools, routing traffic through multiple servers to hide the attacker's real location. Together with compromised servers and botnets, these techniques form a complex, difficult-to-trace infrastructure that seriously hinders efforts to investigate and disrupt phishing campaigns.

The financial incentives driving the development and use of these sophisticated tools are substantial. Phishing kits can be purchased on the dark web at relatively low prices, making them accessible to a broad range of attackers. The potential returns from successful phishing campaigns are significantly higher, encouraging the ongoing development and refinement of these tools. This arms race between attackers and defenders is a constant cycle, with attackers constantly seeking ways to improve their techniques and bypass security measures.

The fight against advanced phishing techniques demands a multi-pronged approach. This includes improving email security measures, educating users about phishing dangers, and investing in robust cybersecurity infrastructure to spot and stop these attacks. Law enforcement and cybersecurity researchers must keep collaborating to identify and disrupt attacker infrastructure, including the takedown of phishing websites and the dismantling of botnets. International cooperation is key, given the global scale of these attacks. The sheer scale and complexity of the problem requires a concerted effort from all stakeholders – individuals, organizations, governments, and technology companies – to combat the ever-evolving phishing threat. Ignoring the sophistication of the tools and infrastructure behind these attacks is a dangerous oversight; fully understanding the attacker's arsenal is crucial to building a strong defense.

Beyond the technical aspects, there's a significant psychological element to the effectiveness of phishing kits.

The attackers aren't just leveraging technological prowess; they're exploiting human psychology. These kits are often designed to prey on common human biases like the desire for convenience, trust in authority, and fear of missing out. Using personalized information and urgent messaging increases the likelihood that a victim will fall prey to a phishing attack.

Understanding these psychological factors is crucial for developing effective countermeasures. Security awareness training programs need to address not just the technical aspects of phishing but also the psychological vulnerabilities that attackers exploit.

The ongoing evolution of phishing techniques, fueled by sophisticated tools and accessible infrastructure, poses a constant challenge for security professionals. The simplicity of phishing kits lowers the barrier to entry for malicious actors, increasing both the volume and sophistication of campaigns. The use of anonymization services, botnets, and geographically dispersed servers makes tracing attacks to their sources extremely difficult. This complexity highlights the need for a comprehensive approach - combining technological advancements in security systems, better user education, and international collaboration to dismantle the supporting infrastructure. The fight against advanced phishing is far from over; it's an ongoing arms race demanding constant vigilance and innovation.

Chapter 22: Detecting and Preventing Advanced Phishing Attacks

Building on the understanding of the sophisticated tools and infrastructure behind advanced phishing attacks, this section focuses on practical methods for detecting and preventing these threats. While easy access to phishing kits lowers the barrier to entry for attackers, knowing how these attacks work helps us develop effective defenses. A layered security approach - combining technical measures with user education and awareness - is crucial for mitigating the risks.

One of the first lines of defense is scrutinizing incoming emails with a critical eye - beyond just glancing at the sender's address. Analyzing email headers can reveal valuable insights into an email's path, revealing potential red flags. Legitimate emails usually follow a clear and consistent chain of mail servers, while suspicious ones may show irregularities, like unexpected hops or servers linked to known malicious activity. Readily available tools online make it easier to exam email headers in detail, presenting the information in a structured and readable format that helps users spot suspicious patterns.

For example, a significant discrepancy between the displayed sender address and the actual sender address (found in the "From" header) is a major warning sign. Similarly, unusual routing information or server IPs associated with spam or phishing operations can often be identified. Learning to effectively interpret email headers empowers users to independently verify the authenticity of incoming messages, reducing their vulnerability to sophisticated phishing attacks.

Beyond headers, the content of the email itself needs careful examination. Malicious links, disguised to appear legitimate, are a cornerstone of many phishing attempts. Instead of directly clicking a link, hovering the mouse cursor over the link typically reveals the actual URL in a tooltip. This simple action lets users compare the displayed URL with the actual destination, revealing discrepancies that might indicate a malicious link. This method works well for simple obfuscation techniques. However, more sophisticated attacks may use URL shortening services or cloaking methods to mask the true destination. In such cases, additional tools can be employed. Many web browsers have extensions specifically designed to analyze URLs and detect potential threats, identifying links associated with known phishing sites or malware distributors. These extensions often check URLs against blacklists maintained by reputable security companies and provide a risk assessment for each link, alerting users to potentially harmful destinations. A cautious approach advises against clicking any link that raises even slight suspicion.

The same level of scrutiny should be applied to email attachments. Opening attachments from unknown or untrusted sources carries significant risk, potentially unleashing malware onto a user's system. Rather than opening an attachment directly, a safer approach involves using a sandbox environment. Sandboxing is a technique that isolates the attachment from the user's main system, allowing it to execute in a controlled environment where it cannot cause damage. Many security software products include built-in sandboxing capabilities, allowing users to safely examine suspicious attachments. If sandboxing isn't available, using a virtual machine provides comparable protection. Virtual machines create a virtualized computing environment separate from the host system, offering a safe space to analyze potentially malicious attachments without risking the integrity of the primary system. Once opened within the sandbox or virtual machine, the attachment's behavior can be closely monitored. Unusual activity, such as unauthorized network connections or attempts to access system files, are clear indicators of malicious intent. Additionally, using reputable antivirus software and keeping it updated is crucial in identifying and blocking malware that might be embedded within attachments.

Advanced phishing attacks often leverage spear-phishing techniques, targeting specific individuals or organizations with highly personalized emails. These attacks exploit social engineering principles, using carefully crafted messages designed to manipulate human biases and vulnerabilities.

Understanding these techniques and recognizing the warning signs is essential for effective prevention. Such emails often contain details seemingly known only to the recipient, increasing the message's credibility and tricking them into revealing sensitive information. However, it's important to remain skeptical, even when presented with seemingly personal details. Cross-checking information and verifying the legitimacy of any request are crucial measures.

Furthermore, many organizations implement security awareness training programs to educate employees about the common tactics used in spear-phishing attacks. These programs often include simulated phishing attacks to help employees recognize and report suspicious emails. Such proactive training significantly improves an organization's ability to prevent successful spear-phishing attempts.

Beyond individual vigilance, implementing robust security measures at the organizational level is critical. Employing multi-factor authentication (MFA) for all online accounts adds a crucial layer of security, making it significantly harder for attackers to gain unauthorized access. MFA requires users to provide two or more forms of authentication, greatly increasing the difficulty for attackers to compromise accounts, even if passwords are obtained. Implementing strong password policies, enforcing regular password changes, and using password managers to securely store credentials also play a vital role. These measures limit the impact of successful phishing attacks by preventing access even when credentials are compromised. Regular security audits and penetration testing help identify vulnerabilities in an organization's systems, enabling proactive remediation. Moreover, regularly updating software and applying security patches is crucial to mitigate the risk of known exploits. This ongoing maintenance is essential for maintaining a high level of security.

Another crucial aspect of advanced phishing attack prevention involves proactively monitoring network traffic and analyzing unusual activity. Intrusion detection systems (IDS) and intrusion prevention systems (IPS) analyze network traffic to identify and block malicious activities. These systems serve as an early warning mechanism, preventing malicious traffic from reaching end-users. Security information and event management (SIEM) systems collect and analyze logs from various security tools, providing a comprehensive view of security events across the organization. SIEM systems can detect patterns indicative of phishing attacks, such as sudden spikes in login attempts from unusual locations or the use of compromised credentials. The use of these advanced tools is often the difference between immediate detection and a successful compromise.

In conclusion, the fight against advanced phishing attacks requires a multifaceted approach. It's not simply about technological solutions, but a combination of technical measures, user education, and a commitment to building a robust security posture. By understanding the technical underpinnings of these attacks, implementing appropriate security measures, and fostering a culture of security awareness, individuals and organizations can significantly reduce their vulnerability to increasingly sophisticated threats. The continuous evolution of phishing techniques demands constant vigilance and a willingness to adapt, ensuring a layered defense capable of confronting the ever-changing landscape of cybercrime. Only through a collaborative effort involving individuals, organizations, and governments can we effectively combat the ongoing threat of advanced phishing attacks and protect ourselves in the digital age.

Chapter 23: Case Studies – Advanced Phishing Campaigns

The previous sections outlined the technical intricacies and preventative measures surrounding advanced phishing techniques. To further solidify this understanding, let's explore several real-world case studies that illustrate the diverse tactics used in sophisticated phishing campaigns.

These examples highlight not only the ingenuity of the attackers but also underscore the critical need for robust security protocols and heightened user awareness.

CASE STUDY #1

Our first case study involves a spear-phishing campaign targeting a major financial institution. The attackers - likely a well-organized cybercrime group - meticulously researched the target's employees, gathering personal information such as names, job titles, and even vacation plans from publicly available social media profiles and company websites. The phishing emails were crafted to appear remarkably authentic, closely mimicking internal communications with a high degree of precision. Subject lines were innocuous, such as "Important Project Update" or "Urgent Travel Itinerary," designed to bypass spam filters and prompt immediate action.

The email content was personalized, referencing specific projects or upcoming events related to the recipient's role within the company. Malicious links were cleverly embedded, disguised as legitimate internal file-sharing services. These links led to meticulously crafted fake login pages, nearly identical to the financial institution's actual portal.

Unsuspecting employees who fell victim to this campaign entered their credentials, unknowingly handing them over directly to the attackers. The impact was significant, resulting in the compromise of sensitive employee and customer data. The attackers gained access to internal systems, potentially exposing financial information, intellectual property, and confidential client records.

This case underscores the potency of spear-phishing attacks when paired with detailed reconnaissance and highly personalized messaging. The attackers' success demonstrates the vulnerability of even sophisticated organizations to socially engineered threats that bypass technical security measures by exploiting human psychology.

The financial institution's response involved a swift incident response plan, including immediate system lockdown, forensic analysis, and notification of affected parties. This highlights the importance of well-defined incident response protocols, including regular security awareness training, in mitigating the impact of such targeted attacks.

CASE STUDY #2

Our second case study focuses on a whaling attack targeting the CEO of a large technology company. Whaling, a more targeted form of spear-phishing, specifically targets high-profile individuals within an organization. In this instance, the attackers used advanced techniques to compromise the CEO's email account - likely by exploiting vulnerabilities in the company's email infrastructure or through sophisticated social engineering to obtain the CEO's credentials.

Once inside, the attackers carefully monitored the CEO's email activity, observing communication patterns and gaining insight into ongoing business dealings. This reconnaissance phase was critical to the success of their subsequent attack. The attackers then crafted an email requesting a large wire transfer, mimicking the legitimate style and tone of a trusted business partner. The message appeared perfectly normal within the context of the CEO's daily communications and raised no suspicion. Unaware of the compromise, the CEO authorized the wire transfer. The attackers swiftly moved a significant sum of money to offshore accounts, leaving little to no trace.

This case highlights the particular dangers associated with whaling attacks. Compromising a high-profile individual's account can lead to devastating financial losses and reputational damage. The absence of obvious technical vulnerabilities makes prevention especially challenging, relying heavily on employee training, multi-factor authentication, and continuous monitoring of suspicious email activity.

The incident served as a major wake-up call, prompting the organization to overhaul its security protocols. Stronger authentication methods were implemented, and employee training programs were enhanced to raise awareness of these targeted attacks. It also emphasizes the critical role of regular security audits and penetration testing in identifying vulnerabilities within an organization's systems and infrastructure.

CASE STUDY #3

A third illustrative case involves a sophisticated phishing campaign using a new variant of malware delivered via an infected Microsoft Office document. The attack began with a seemingly innocuous email claiming to be an urgent invoice from a legitimate supplier. The email included an attachment labelled as an invoice in .docx format. However, the document contained malicious macros that automatically executed upon opening. These macros silently downloaded and installed a new variant of ransomware known as *Crypto malware X*.

This ransomware was especially insidious, encrypting not only the victim's local files but also replicating itself across the network, locking data on other connected systems. This rapid spread compounded the damage significantly. The attackers demanded a substantial ransom in cryptocurrency in exchange for the decryption key. The targeted organization - a mid-sized manufacturing firm – was forced to shut down operations while scrambling to contain the ransomware's spread.

The cost of the recovery far exceeded the initial ransom demand, including data restoration from backups, system reconfiguration, and significant downtime. This case study demonstrates the ever-evolving threat landscape, as attackers continue to refine their techniques and develop malware variants capable of bypassing traditional security defenses.

The success of this attack underscores the importance of regular security updates, employee training on safe file handling, and robust endpoint protection solutions capable of detecting and neutralizing advanced threats. Strong network segmentation, which could have prevented the lateral spread of the malware, would have greatly reduced the impact in this scenario.

These examples are not isolated incidents - they represent only a small fraction of the countless advanced phishing campaigns launched daily across the globe. The common thread running through them is the attackers' exploitation of human vulnerability, coupled with sophisticated technical capabilities.

The methods used - from spear-phishing and whaling to exploiting zero-day software vulnerabilities - highlight the urgent need for multi-layered security strategies. These include robust technical defenses such as strong authentication, up-to-date software, security information and event management (SIEM) systems, and intrusion detection and prevention systems (IDS/IPS).

Equally important, if not more so, is a strong emphasis on user education and awareness training. Employees must be equipped with the knowledge and skills to identify and report suspicious emails and attachments, forming a critical first line of defense.

Only through a combination of technological sophistication and user awareness can we effectively combat the ever-evolving threat of advanced phishing attacks and secure our digital world. The constant development of new attack vectors demands a proactive, adaptable approach to cybersecurity – one that requires constant vigilance and a commitment to adopting the latest security best practices.

The future of cybersecurity will rely on collaboration between individuals, organizations, and governments to maintain a resilient digital landscape, capable of withstanding the persistent pressure of sophisticated cyber-criminals.

Chapter 24: Immediate Actions After a Suspected Phishing Attack

The immediate aftermath of a suspected phishing attack demands swift and decisive action. Delaying your response can significantly increase the potential damage to your personal information, financial accounts, and online reputation.

This section provides a detailed, step-by-step guide to the critical actions you must take as soon as you suspect you've been targeted.

Remember: the goal is to contain the breach, minimize further compromise, and initiate the recovery process.

First and foremost, **disconnect from the internet**. This immediate step cuts off communication with the attacker and limits their ability to install malware or exfiltrate data. Be sure to disconnect all connected devices - including your computer, smartphone, and anything else that might have been exposed.

If you're on a public Wi-Fi network, this step is even more critical. Public networks often lack proper security protocols, leaving your device especially vulnerable to further compromise.

Next, **change all your passwords** - starting with any accounts you believe may have been compromised. This includes email accounts, online banking portals, social media profiles, and any other services where you've used the same or similar passwords.

Use strong, unique passwords for each account. Avoid easily guessable information like birthdays or pet names. A password manager can help securely store and generate complex passwords for you.

Whenever possible, enable multi-factor authentication (MFA) to add an extra layer of protection. MFA requires a second form of verification - such as a one-time code sent to your phone or a biometric scan – making it much harder for attackers to gain access, even if your password is compromised.

Thoroughly **review your financial accounts.** Check your bank accounts, credit card statements, and investment accounts for any unauthorized transactions or unusual activity. Be meticulous - look for even small charges that could indicate a test transaction before a larger theft.

Report any suspicious activity to your bank or financial institution immediately. You may also want to consider placing a fraud alert or security freeze on your credit report to prevent new accounts from being opened in your name. Most credit bureaus offer these services to help protect your financial standing.

Check your devices for malicious software (malware). Run a full system scan using a reputable antivirus program, and make sure it's up-to-date with the latest virus definitions. If malware is detected, remove it immediately following your antivirus program's instructions.

If your antivirus can't fully eliminate the threat, consider using specialized malware removal tools. Some malware is incredibly sophisticated and may evade standard detection – so don't assume your system is clean after just one scan.

Beyond your immediate financial accounts and devices, it's crucial to **examine your connected devices.** Phishing attacks aren't confined to computers - they can also target smartphones, smart TVs, and other connected devices.

Check your smartphone for unusual apps, unexpected activity, or changes in settings. Review smart home devices for unauthorized access or strange behavior. If you suspect a device has been compromised, perform a factory reset to remove any potential malware and restore it to a secure state.

Keep in mind: restoring a device to factory settings will erase all your data on that device. Be sure to back up any important information before proceeding.

Contact your service providers. This step involves notifying relevant authorities and organizations about the suspected phishing attack. Start by contacting your email provider to report the phishing attempt and potentially block or flag the sender's email address.

Inform your bank and credit card companies, especially if you suspect any financial compromise. Reach out to other relevant services - such as social media platforms or online retailers - if you believe your accounts may have been affected.

The more information you provide to these organizations, the better equipped they'll be to respond and help mitigate any potential harm.

Consider **reporting the incident to law enforcement.** Depending on the nature of the attack and the potential damage, you may want to file a report with your local police department or relevant federal agency - such as the Federal Trade Commission (FTC) in the United States, or its equivalent in other countries.

These reports help law enforcement track cybercrime trends and may contribute to investigations that identify and apprehend perpetrators. Even if the financial loss seems minimal, reporting the incident adds to a larger dataset that supports future prevention efforts.

The FTC, for example, offers useful resources and clear reporting mechanisms for phishing-related incidents. Take time to familiarize yourself with the appropriate reporting agencies in your jurisdiction.

Document everything. Keep detailed records of all communications related to the suspected phishing attack - including emails, text messages, and phone calls.

Maintain a detailed log of every action you've taken: note the date and time, the names of individuals or departments you contacted, and the specific steps you took to secure your accounts and devices.

Thorough documentation is essential if the incident requires further investigation or if you need to provide information to law enforcement or service providers. The more organized and detailed your records, the more effective your response will be.

Review and enhance your security practices. After a phishing attack, take steps to strengthen your defenses and reduce the risk of future incidents.

This includes regularly updating your software, using strong and unique passwords, enabling multi-factor authentication (MFA) wherever possible, installing reputable antivirus software, and staying alert to suspicious emails, texts, and calls.

Consider undergoing additional cybersecurity training to deepen your understanding of phishing techniques and scams. Cybercriminals constantly evolve their tactics - staying informed is essential for protecting yourself in today's digital landscape.

Finally, **monitor your accounts and devices.** Even after taking the initial recovery steps, continued to vigilance is crucial.

Keep a close eye on your bank accounts, credit card statements, and other online accounts for any unusual transactions. Regularly scan your devices for malware, and make sure your security software is always up to date.

Ongoing attention is key to preventing long-term damage from a phishing attack. A persistent, proactive approach to online security is essential for mitigating the risks posed by sophisticated phishing campaigns.

The steps outlined here are not exhaustive; the specific actions you take will depend on the circumstances of the suspected phishing attack. However, by following these guidelines and responding swiftly, you can significantly reduce the potential impact and protect your valuable personal and financial information.

Proactive measures - coupled with a prompt, decisive action - are your best defenses against this ever-evolving threat. Consistent vigilance and a commitment to strong security practices are essential in navigating the complexities of today's digital world.

The cost of inaction often far outweighs the effort required to respond quickly. When it comes to phishing attacks, speed and strategy are your best allies.

Chapter 25: Reporting Phishing Attempts to Authorities

Reporting a phishing attempt might seem like a minor inconvenience, especially if there's no immediate financial loss. However, failing to report these incidents significantly hinders efforts to combat cybercrime.

Each report contributes to a larger dataset that helps law enforcement agencies, internet service providers (ISPs), and cybersecurity firms identify trends, track down perpetrators, and develop more effective preventative measures.

Your report adds valuable intelligence to the fight – information that can help protect countless others from falling victim to similar attacks.

The process of reporting a phishing attempt involves several key steps, starting with identifying the appropriate authorities. The first point of contact often depends on the nature of the attack. If the phishing email targeted your bank account, for example, your priority should be contacting your bank's fraud department.

Provide them with the phishing email, the sender's information (if available), and any other relevant details. Be prepared to answer questions about the email's content, your response, and any suspicious activity on your account. The bank's fraud department is equipped to handle these situations and can take steps to secure your account and investigate the fraudulent activity.

Similarly, if the phishing attempt targeted a specific online service – such as a social media platform or an online retailer - contact their customer support or security team immediately. Most reputable services have established procedures for reporting phishing attempts. Their security teams are trained to identify and address these threats and can take action to prevent further attacks.

Be sure to document the date, time, and content of the phishing attempt. Save any relevant emails, text messages, or screenshots of the fraudulent website. This information will be essential in the reporting process and for any subsequent investigation.

Beyond contacting the specific service provider, consider reporting the incident to your Internet Service Provider (ISP). Your ISP can help block the sender's email address or IP address, preventing further phishing attempts from the same source. They may also have internal security measures to identify and mitigate threats originating within their network. Many ISPs offer resources and support for customers experiencing cyberattacks, and they can provide guidance on additional security measures to protect your account. Be sure to explain the situation clearly, including details about the phishing email, the sender, and any relevant links or attachments.

In many jurisdictions, reporting phishing attempts to law enforcement is crucial, even if there's no immediate financial loss. The information you provide contributes to a broader understanding of cybercrime trends, enabling law enforcement agencies to develop more effective prevention and prosecution strategies. In the United States, the Federal Trade Commission (FTC) is a key resource for reporting phishing scams. The FTC maintains an online reporting system that makes it easy for individuals to submit details of phishing attempts. The information submitted helps the FTC track phishing campaigns, identify emerging threats, alert consumers about prevalent phishing scams - boosting overall digital literacy and user safety.

Similar agencies exist in other countries. For instance, in the United Kingdom, Action Fraud is the national reporting center for fraud and cybercrime. In Canada, the Canadian Anti-Fraud Centre (CAFC) plays a similar role, providing a central point for individuals to report various types of fraud, including phishing scams. These agencies often collaborate internationally to track and apprehend cybercriminals operating across borders. Reports from individuals form the crucial groundwork for these collaborative investigations.

When reporting to law enforcement, be as detailed as possible. This includes providing the following information:

The date and time of the phishing attempt: Precise timestamps help establish a timeline of events.

The sender's email address or phone number: This is crucial for identifying the source of the attack. Note any variations or potentially associated accounts.

The content of the phishing email or message: Include quotes from the email or screenshots of any suspicious websites.

Any links or attachments: Do not click on these links; instead, provide the URLs to the authorities.

Any actions you took in response: Describe how you responded to the phishing attempt and any steps you've taken to secure your accounts.

Any financial losses or damages: Clearly articulate any financial losses or damages suffered as a result of the incident. Keep detailed records of transactions and any communication with your financial institutions.

Screenshots and digital evidence: Screenshots of the phishing email, the fraudulent website, and any other relevant digital evidence are incredibly valuable.

Details of any affected accounts: Identify any online accounts or services that might have been targeted.

Remember that your report contributes to a larger effort in combating cybercrime. By providing detailed information to the appropriate authorities, you're not only protecting yourself but also helping make the internet a safer place for everyone. The collective action of reporting these incidents, combined with proactive security measures, significantly strengthens our defenses against sophisticated phishing campaigns.

Beyond the immediate reporting, maintaining comprehensive documentation is crucial. Keep records of all communications with authorities - including email confirmations, case numbers, and any other relevant information. This detailed record will be essential if further action is required, such as providing evidence for insurance claims or assisting law enforcement in their investigations.

This documentation also serves as a valuable resource for your personal records, allowing you to track the progress of your report and understand the process involved in reporting cybercrime.

In conclusion, reporting phishing attempts is a crucial step in protecting yourself and the broader digital community. By promptly contacting the appropriate authorities and providing detailed information, you contribute to a collective effort in identifying, tracking, and ultimately preventing these sophisticated attacks. Remember to meticulously document every aspect of the incident - from the initial phishing attempt to your interactions with various agencies.

This thorough documentation ensures a smooth reporting process and allows for more effective action to be taken against cybercriminals. The investment of time and effort in reporting significantly outweighs the potential risks associated with inaction, contributing to a safer, more secure digital environment for all.

Chapter 26: Mitigating Potential Damage

The aftermath of a successful phishing attack can feel overwhelming, but swift and decisive action can significantly minimize the damage. The immediate priority is to contain the breach and prevent further exploitation of your compromised information. This involves several crucial steps, each designed to secure your accounts, protect your financial assets, and safeguard your personal identity.

First, secure your accounts. If the phishing attack targeted a specific online account - such as your email, banking, or social media account - change your password immediately. Don't just choose a new password; select a strong, unique password that's different from any others you use. A strong password incorporates a mix of uppercase and lowercase letters, numbers, and symbols. Consider using a password manager to securely store and manage your complex passwords. Many reputable password managers offer features that generate strong, unique passwords for each of your online accounts.

Beyond simply changing your passwords, consider enabling two-factor authentication (2FA) wherever possible. 2FA adds an extra layer of security by requiring a second form of verification - such as a code sent to your phone or email - in addition to your password. This makes it exponentially more difficult for attackers to access your accounts, even if they've obtained your password. This applies to all your critical online account: banking, email, social media, online shopping—basically anything that holds sensitive information.

If the phishing email contained malware or malicious links, immediately run a full system scan with your antivirus or anti-malware software. Ensure your software is up-to-date and that you're running a thorough scan to identify and remove any malicious files or programs that may have been installed. Depending on the type of malware involved, you might need to take more drastic steps, such as reinstalling your operating system. If you're unsure how to handle this, consider contacting a computer professional for assistance - professional help might save you from more significant damage down the line.

Protecting your finances is the next critical step. If you suspect that your bank account or credit card information has been compromised, contact your financial institution immediately. Report the incident and request that they place a fraud alert on your accounts - this will help prevent unauthorized transactions. Many banks offer proactive fraud monitoring, which can alert you to any suspicious activity on your accounts. Take advantage of such services. Regularly check your bank and credit card statements for any unauthorized transactions. Don't just rely on automated alerts - scrutinize your statements carefully.

Consider placing a freeze on your credit reports. A credit freeze prevents anyone from accessing your credit report without your explicit permission, making it much more difficult for identity thieves to open new accounts or take out loans in your name. You can place a freeze with each of the three major credit bureaus: Equifax, Experian, and TransUnion. While a credit freeze might slightly inconvenience you when you need to apply for credit, the protection it offers against identity theft far outweighs any minor inconvenience.

Monitor your financial transactions closely. Review your bank and credit card statements regularly for any unauthorized activity and be especially vigilant in the weeks and months following the phishing attack. Any suspicious transactions should be reported to your financial institution immediately. Keep detailed records of all your transactions, including dates, amounts, and merchants. This will assist in any investigations, should they become necessary, and help you manage the process of reclaiming any funds.

Addressing potential identity theft is crucial. Phishing attacks often aim to steal personal information that can be used for identity theft. To mitigate this risk, consider placing a fraud alert or security freeze on your credit reports.

Monitor your credit reports regularly for any unauthorized accounts or inquiries. Most credit bureaus offer free credit reports, and you should take advantage of these services —especially after a suspected data breach.

Beyond credit monitoring, review your online accounts for any unusual activity. Check your email, social media accounts, and other online services for any suspicious logins or password changes. If you discover anything unusual, change your passwords immediately and report the incident to the relevant service provider. Be cautious about clicking links or opening attachments in unexpected emails - these could lead to additional malware or phishing attempts.

Restore affected systems. If the phishing attack compromised your computer or mobile device, take steps to restore it to a clean state. This might involve reinstalling your operating system, restoring your device from a backup, or wiping the device completely. Before reinstalling the operating system, back up any important data that isn't already backed up to avoid losing irretrievable information. If the restoration process is complex, consider seeking help from a computer professional - especially if you're concerned about residual malware or other threats

The process of recovering from a phishing attack can be complex and time-consuming. However, by taking swift action to secure your accounts, monitor your financial transactions, and protect against identity theft, you can significantly mitigate the potential damage. Remember, prevention is always the best defense. Stay vigilant, practice safe online habits, and stay informed about emerging cybersecurity threats. Regularly update your software, use strong passwords, and enable two-factor authentication whenever possible. These proactive measures go a long way in reducing your vulnerability to phishing attacks and other forms of cybercrime.

Remember that the emotional toll of a phishing attack can be significant. Feeling violated or frustrated is common. Don't hesitate to seek support from friends, family, or mental health professionals if you need help processing the experience. Taking care of your emotional well-being is just as crucial as protecting your digital security.

Finally, consider educating yourself further on cybersecurity best practices. Numerous online resources, books, and courses are available to help you learn more about identifying and avoiding phishing attempts, as well as protecting your personal information online. The time you invest in improving your digital literacy is an investment in your long-term security and peace of mind. Staying informed and proactive is the best way to safeguard yourself in the ever-evolving world of cyber threats. By combining prompt response, meticulous recovery, and continuous education, you can significantly reduce your vulnerability and build a stronger defense against the increasing sophistication of phishing attacks.

Chapter 27: Legal and Financial Recourse

The emotional and practical aftermath of a phishing attack extends beyond immediate account security and financial safeguards. Understanding your legal and financial recourse is crucial for regaining control and potentially recovering losses. This section explores the avenues available to victims, emphasizing the importance of meticulous documentation and proactive engagement with legal and financial institutions.

First, it's vital to understand that you are not alone. Phishing attacks are a widespread problem, and many legal and regulatory frameworks exist to protect victims. The specific laws and procedures may vary depending on your location (country, state, etc.), the nature of the attack, and the extent of the damages suffered. However, several common threads unite victims' rights globally. These rights often include the right to report the crime to the appropriate authorities, access information about the attack and its potential impact, and seek compensation for any losses incurred.

One of the most critical initial steps is comprehensive documentation. This meticulous record-keeping serves as the foundation for any subsequent legal or financial claim. Begin by gathering all relevant information related to the phishing attack. This includes:

The phishing communication itself: Save copies of the emails, text messages, or phone call recordings. Note the sender's details, the subject line, the content of the message, and any links or attachments. If possible, preserve the original headers and metadata of emails, as this information can be crucial in identifying the source of the attack. Screenshots are also valuable evidence.

Records of financial transactions: This includes bank statements, credit card statements, and any other records showing unauthorized transactions or withdrawals. Keep detailed records of all communication with your financial institutions regarding the incident. This documentation helps track the timeline of events and establish the extent of your financial losses.

Copies of identification documents: If your personal information was compromised, gather copies of your driver's license, passport, Social Security card, and other identification documents. This is vital if you need to file a police report or report identity theft to credit bureaus.

Communication with service providers: Maintain records of all interactions with banks, credit card companies, social media platforms, and other online services affected by the phishing attack. Keep records of your requests for account recovery, fraud alerts, and any other services you've received.

Expert reports (if applicable): If you've hired a cybersecurity professional or forensic investigator to analyze the attack, keep copies of their reports. These reports provide independent verification of the attack and can be critical evidence in legal proceedings.

These documents provide a comprehensive history of the event. This detailed chronology supports your claims for compensation and helps investigators trace the source of the attack. In the digital world, evidence can be easily lost or altered, so proactive and meticulous record-keeping is paramount. Use a secure, organized system to store these documents - preferably offline and in a physically secure location.

Once you have documented the phishing attack, promptly report the incident to the appropriate authorities. This typically includes the police, your financial institutions, and the relevant online service providers. The police report will help establish a record of the crime, which may be necessary for insurance claims or legal action. Your financial institutions will investigate any unauthorized transactions and may offer compensation or remediation. Reporting to online service providers allows them to take action against the attackers and prevent similar attacks in the future.

Consider filing a complaint with the Federal Trade Commission (FTC) in the United States, or the equivalent agency in your country. The FTC maintains a database of consumer complaints that helps identify trends in cybercrime and take action against perpetrators. This reporting also forms future preventative measures. For example, identifying a specific phishing campaign helps companies and agencies strengthen cybersecurity defenses against such attacks. Your report contributes to this crucial data.

Depending on the nature and extent of the damage caused by the phishing attack, you may wish to consider pursuing legal action. This might involve filing a lawsuit against the perpetrators of the attack or against the organization that failed to adequately protect your data. However, pursuing legal action should be done with careful consideration and the assistance of legal counsel. Legal cases can be complex, time-consuming, and costly, and the outcome is never guaranteed. Still, in cases of significant financial losses or identity theft, the potential benefits of legal action often outweigh the costs.

Choosing the right legal counsel is paramount. Seek a lawyer specializing in cybercrime, data breaches, or consumer protection. An experienced lawyer will understand the complexities of these cases and be able to navigate the legal system effectively. Many lawyers offer free initial consultations, allowing you to discuss your case and assess the viability of legal action. Don't hesitate to contact multiple lawyers to find the one best suited to your needs.

Beyond legal recourse, understanding your rights under financial protection laws is crucial. For instance, many countries have laws that protect consumers from unauthorized transactions and fraud. Under the Fair Credit Billing Act in the U.S., consumers have specific rights to dispute unauthorized charges on their credit card accounts. Similar laws exist in many other countries, offering protection against financial losses resulting from phishing attacks. Reviewing and fully understanding your rights is essential in the claims process.

Your financial institution also plays a critical role. Banks and credit card companies generally have policies and procedures for handling fraud claims. Contact your bank or credit card company immediately if you suspect unauthorized activity on your accounts. They will guide you through their specific processes for reporting fraud, investigating the incident, and potentially refunding your losses. They are typically obligated to investigate thoroughly and may reverse fraudulent transactions.

Document all communications with them, retain copies of any correspondence, and transaction records.

Remember, navigating the legal and financial aftermath of a phishing attack requires patience, persistence, and meticulous record-keeping. The process might be lengthy and complex, but by understanding your rights and pursuing available avenues of recourse, you can increase your chances of recovering your losses and protecting yourself from future attacks. Proactive steps - such as securing your accounts immediately after an attack, reporting the incident to the relevant authorities, and documenting all relevant information - can significantly enhance your chances of a successful outcome. It's a journey that demands both emotional resilience and strategic planning. Seeking professional assistance, whether legal or financial, can greatly facilitate this process and improve your chances of recovery.

Chapter 28: Rebuilding Trust and Preventing Future Attacks

Rebuilding trust after a phishing attack is a crucial - and often overlooked - step in the recovery process. The emotional toll can be significant, leading to feelings of vulnerability, anxiety, and even shame. It's vital to acknowledge these feelings and understand that you are not alone. Millions of people experience phishing attacks each year, and the experience is often unsettling. The first step toward rebuilding trust is acknowledging your emotions and recognizing that being targeted is not a reflection of your intelligence or competence. Phishing attacks are sophisticated, and even the most tech-savvy individuals can fall victim.

This sense of vulnerability, however, can be addressed proactively. One key aspect of regaining control is taking concrete steps to improve your digital security posture. This involves more than just changing passwords; it requires a comprehensive reassessment of your online habits and security practices. Begin by reviewing all your online accounts. Change passwords for any accounts that may have been compromised, including email, social media, banking, and shopping accounts. Don't reuse passwords across different platforms - this is a critical security vulnerability.

Consider using a password manager to generate strong, unique passwords for each account. These tools can significantly reduce the risk of future compromises.

Beyond password management, reassess your email security settings. Enable two-factor authentication (2FA) wherever possible. This adds an extra layer of security by requiring a second verification method - such as a code sent to your phone - in addition to your password. This makes it significantly harder for attackers to access your accounts, even if they obtain your password. Regularly review your email inbox for suspicious messages, paying close attention to sender addresses, links, and attachments. Be wary of emails that request personal information, demand urgent action, or contain unusual formatting or grammar. If an email seems even slightly suspicious, do not click on any links or open any attachments.

Educate yourself on the latest phishing techniques. Cybercriminals constantly evolve their methods, so staying informed is essential. Subscribe to reputable cybersecurity blogs and newsletters to stay up-to-date on current threats and best practices. Many organizations and government agencies offer free resources and training on identifying and avoiding phishing attacks. Understanding the techniques used by attackers can help you become more vigilant and better equipped to spot suspicious communications. The knowledge you gain can empower you, reducing the fear of falling prey to future attacks. The shift is from reactive recovery to proactive prevention.

Strengthen your overall online security by keeping your software updated. Regularly update your operating system, web browser, and antivirus software. These updates often include security patches that fix known vulnerabilities, making your devices less susceptible to attacks. Be cautious when clicking on links or downloading files from unfamiliar sources. Only download software from trusted websites and reputable app stores. Avoid using public Wi-Fi networks for sensitive transactions, as these networks can be easily intercepted by attackers. If you must use public Wi-Fi, use a virtual private network (VPN) to encrypt your data and protect your privacy.

Furthermore, foster a culture of security within your family and social circles. Talk to your friends, family, and colleagues about phishing attacks and the importance of online safety. Share tips and resources on how to identify and avoid scams. By promoting awareness, you contribute to a broader community effort to combat phishing and other cybercrimes. Collective understanding and awareness help build a more resilient digital environment for everyone.

Beyond technical security measures, consider developing a more cautious and discerning approach to online communication. Don't rush into clicking links or providing information - take your time and carefully scrutinize any requests. Always verify the authenticity of communication, especially if it seems urgent or unexpected. If you're unsure about the legitimacy of an email or message, contact the sender directly using a known contact number or email address rather than replying to the suspicious communication.

This heightened awareness extends beyond email to other communication channels. Be cautious of suspicious text messages (smishing) and phone calls (vishing). These attacks are becoming increasingly sophisticated, often using social engineering techniques to manipulate victims. Never reveal personal information over the phone or via text message unless you are absolutely certain of the recipient's identity. If a caller claims to represent a legitimate organization, hang up and independently verify their identity using a known contact number or the organization's official website.

Remember, regaining trust is a process. It requires a combination of technical improvements, behavioral changes, and emotional resilience. Give yourself time to recover from the emotional impact of the phishing attack.

Focus on the steps you're taking to improve your digital security. Each measure you implement is a testament to your proactive commitment to personal safety. It's a journey of continuous learning and adaptation, requiring ongoing vigilance in the face of ever-evolving threats.

Beyond individual actions, consider reporting the phishing attempt. Report the suspicious email, text message, or phone call to the appropriate authorities, such as the Federal Trade Commission (FTC) in the United States or the equivalent agency in your country. Doing so not only helps protect you, but also contributes to the broader effort to combat phishing.

Your report may aid in identifying and prosecuting perpetrators, directly contributing to the prevention of future attacks. This collective action is crucial in the fight against phishing.

Finally, celebrate your progress. Acknowledging and appreciating the steps you've taken to enhance your security builds confidence and reinforces positive habits. Successfully navigating a phishing attack should empower you to engage more confidently and securely in the digital world. Remember, resilience is built through continuous learning and adaptation. Each time you avoid a phishing attempt, your sense of security and competence grows. This positive feedback loop is critical to maintaining a strong, robust defense against future threats. The goal isn't to live in fear, but to live with informed awareness and proactive security practices. The digital world offers immense benefits, and with the right approach, you can navigate it safely and confidently.

Acknowledgements

I am deeply grateful to the many individuals who contributed to the creation of this book. First and foremost, I want to thank my editors, Veronica Goldspiel and Michelle Kulp, for their guidance, patience, and unwavering support throughout the writing process. Their insights and expertise were invaluable in shaping the final manuscript.

I also extend my sincere appreciation to the Red Rabbit Security team, whose contributions significantly enhanced the accuracy and clarity of the book.

Special thanks go to Lucy, Eddie, Mike, Roman, and Eric for their understanding and encouragement during the long hours spent researching and writing.

Finally, I acknowledge the countless victims of phishing, smishing, and vishing scams, whose experiences inspired this book and underscored the urgent need for accessible and practical guidance on digital security.

Appendix

This appendix contains supplementary resources to further enhance your understanding of phishing, smishing, and vishing attacks.

A.1: List of Reporting Agencies: This section provides a comprehensive list of national and international agencies responsible for reporting cybercrimes, including contact information and relevant websites for each jurisdiction.

US – UNITED STATES AGENCIES

- **Internet Crime Complaint Center (IC3)**

    - Purpose: Central hub for reporting cyber-enabled crimes.
    - Website: ic3.gov
    - Contact: Submit complaints online.
    - staysafeonline.org

- **Federal Bureau of Investigation (FBI) – Cyber Division**

    - Purpose: Investigates cyber threats and crimes.

- Website: fbi.gov/investigate/cyber
- Contact: Submit tips at tips.fbi.gov or call 1-800-CALL-FBI (225-5324).

- **Cybersecurity and Infrastructure Security Agency (CISA)**

  - Purpose: Provides cybersecurity resources and incident response.
  - Website: cisa.gov
  - Contact: Email central@cisa.gov or call 888-282-0870.

- **U.S. Secret Service – Cyber Fraud Task Forces**

  - Purpose: Investigates cyber-enabled financial crimes.
  - Website: secretservice.gov/investigations/cyber
  - Contact: Contact local field offices.

- **Federal Trade Commission (FTC)**

  - Purpose: Handles consumer complaints, including identity theft.
  - Website: identitytheft.gov
  - Contact: Call 1-877-IDTHEFT (1-877-438-4338).

INTERNATIONAL AGENCIES

- **INTERPOL – Cybercrime Directorate**

    - Purpose: Facilitates international police cooperation against cybercrime.
    - Website: interpol.int/Crimes/Cybercrime
    - Contact: Through national INTERPOL offices.

- **Europol – European Cybercrime Centre (EC3)**

    - Purpose: Coordinates EU law enforcement against cybercrime.
    - Website: europol.europa.eu
    - Contact: Via national law enforcement agencies.

UK – UNITED KINGDOM AGENCIES

- **National Cyber Security Centre (NCSC)**

    - Purpose: Provides cybersecurity guidance and incident response.
    - Website: ncsc.gov.uk
    - Contact: Report incidents via the website.

CA – CANADA AGENCIES

- **Canadian Centre for Cyber Security**

    - Purpose: National authority on cybersecurity.

    - Website: cyber.gc.ca

    - Contact: Report incidents via the website.

AU – AUSTRALIA AGENCIES

- **Australian Cyber Security Centre (ACSC)**

    - Purpose: Leads the Australian Government's efforts on cybersecurity.

    - Website: cyber.gov.au

    - Contact: Report incidents via the website.

IN – INDIA AGENCIES

- **Indian Computer Emergency Response Team (CERT-In)**

    - Purpose: Handles cybersecurity incidents and provides alerts.

    - Website: cert-in.org.in

    - Contact: Email incident@cert-in.org.in.

GR - GREECE AGENCIES

- **Cyber Crime Division – Hellenic Police**

- Purpose: Investigates cybercrimes within Greece.

- Website: cyberalert.gr

- Contact: Call 11188 or email ccu@cybercrimeunit.gr.

IT – ITALY AGENCIES

- **Polizia Postale e delle Comunicazioni**

  - Purpose: Handles cybercrime and communications-related offenses.

  - Website: poliziadistato.it

  - Contact: Contact local offices via the website.

A.2: Sample Phishing Emails: This section includes examples of various phishing email templates, showcasing the diverse tactics used by cybercriminals. These examples are provided for educational purposes only and should not be considered exhaustive.

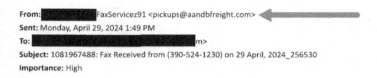

A screenshot of a email

AI-generated content may be incorrect.

PHISHING, VISHING, AND SMISHING... OH MY!

From: Community Bank <shara.samarita@edgehomefinance.com>
Sent: Monday, April 8, 2024 2:14 PM
Subject: Action Requested-You have received secure document on Monday 04/08/2024.

Attachments: Secure Document.zip

This is your requested security alert notification.

You have received secure document on Monday 04/08/2024.

Please note that once a secure document has been notarized it is only valid for limited time.

We strongly recommend you download the secure document from the attached and review before your document expire

Thank you for banking with Community Bank, N.A

This email was generated automatically. Please do not reply to this message.

A screenshot of a email

AI-generated content may be incorrect.

A.3: Additional Online Resources: This section lists trusted websites and organizations that offer valuable information on online safety and security best practices.

GLOBAL RESOURCES

- **Cybersecurity & Infrastructure Security Agency (CISA)**

    - U.S. federal agency providing alerts, toolkits, and best practices for protecting infrastructure.

    - Topics: phishing, ransomware, critical infrastructure, small business security.

- **National Cyber Security Centre (UK)**

    - UK's national authority on cybersecurity.

    - Resources: Cyber Aware campaign, guidance for SMBs, and technical advisories.

- **StaySafeOnline.org – National Cybersecurity Alliance**

    - U.S.-based public/private partnership offering easy-to-understand resources for individuals and businesses.

    - Topics: password hygiene, social engineering, remote work security.

- **Europol EC3 – European Cybercrime Centre**

  - Provides international alerts and resources related to cybercrime trends.

  - Topics: ransomware, financial fraud, cybercrime reports.

- **ENISA – EU Agency for Cybersecurity**

  - Offers policy support, awareness campaigns, and practical cybersecurity toolkits.

  - Publications: Threat Landscape Reports, cloud security guides.

U.S. SPECIFIC RESOURCES

- **Federal Trade Commission (FTC)**

  - Consumer-focused tips on privacy, scams, and identity theft.

  - Topics: scam alerts, reporting fraud, data breaches.

- **FBI Cyber Division**

  - Investigation summaries, alerts, and guidance on reporting cyber incidents.

  - Topics: cybercrime, business email compromise, national security threats.

- **SANS Internet Storm Center**

  - Community-driven threat intelligence and daily cybersecurity updates.

  - Audience: IT pros, SOC analysts, and researchers.

EDUCATIONAL AND OPEN-SOURCE INITIATIVES

- **Krebs on Security**

  - Independent journalist Brian Krebs' blog on cyber threats and real-world breaches.

  - Topics: malware, DDoS, fraud, breaches.

- **CyberAware.gov.au – ACSC (Australia)**

  - Australia's national cybersecurity hub for citizens and small businesses.

- **Have I Been Pwned**

  - Free tool to check if your email or password has been exposed in a data breach.

- **Mozilla Foundation Internet Health**

  - Research and advocacy around open, safe, and private internet practices.

FOR SMALL AND MEDIUM-SIZED BUSINESSES (SMBs)

- **FCC Small Biz Cyber Planner**

  - Build-your-own cyber plan template tailored for SMBs.

- **NIST Cybersecurity Framework**

  - A widely adopted framework for improving critical infrastructure and small business security posture.

- **Red Rabbit Security (If you're looking for managed cybersecurity services)**

  - Website: Redrabbitsec.com

  - Subscription-based security solutions for SMBs, with guidance on compliance, phishing defense, and breach prevention.

Glossary

2FA (Two-Factor Authentication): A security process that requires two separate forms of authentication to verify a user's identity.

Antivirus Software: Software designed to detect and remove malicious software (malware).

Cybercrime: Criminal activities carried out through electronic means, such as phishing or hacking.

Data Breach: A security incident where sensitive data is stolen or compromised.

Malware: Malicious software designed to damage, disrupt, or gain unauthorized access to a computer system.

Phishing: A cybercrime where attackers attempt to trick individuals into revealing sensitive information through deceptive emails, websites, or messages.

Smishing: Phishing attacks carried out via text message (SMS).

Social Engineering: Manipulative techniques used to trick individuals into divulging confidential information or performing actions that compromise security.

Vishing: Phishing attacks conducted over the telephone.

VPN (Virtual Private Network): A technology that creates a secure, encrypted connection over a public network, such as the internet.

References

Federal Bureau of Investigation. (2023). *Internet Crime Report 2022*. FBI Internet Crime Complaint Center (IC3). https://www.ic3.gov/Media/PDF/AnnualReport/2022_IC3Report.pdf

Verizon. (2023). *2023 Data Breach Investigations Report*. Verizon Communications. https://www.verizon.com/business/resources/reports/dbir/

Hadnagy, C. (2018). *Social Engineering: The science of human hacking* (2nd ed.). Wiley.

Jakobsson, M., & Myers, S. (2006). *Phishing and countermeasures: Understanding the increasing problem of electronic identity theft*. Wiley-Interscience.

Symantec. (2021). *Internet Security Threat Report, Volume 26*. NortonLifeLock. https://symantec-enterprise-blogs.security.com/

Alsharnouby, M., Alaca, F., & Chiasson, S. (2015). Why phishing still works: User strategies for combating phishing attacks. *Inter-

national Journal of Human-Computer Studies, 82, 69–82. https://doi.org/10.1016/j.ijhcs.2015.05.005

Twitchell, D. P., & Adkins, M. (2019). A taxonomy and knowledge sharing model for smishing attacks. *Journal of Cybersecurity Education, Research and Practice, 2019*(1), Article 5. https://digitalcommons.kennesaw.edu/jcerp/vol2019/iss1/5

Proofpoint. (2023). *State of the Phish Report 2023.* https://www.proofpoint.com/us/resources/threat-reports/state-of-phish

O'Hara, K., & Shadbolt, N. (2020). *The spy in the coffee machine: The end of privacy as we know it* (2nd ed.). Oneworld Publications.

ENISA – European Union Agency for Cybersecurity. (2023). *Threat Landscape 2023.* https://www.enisa.europa.eu/publications/enisa-threat-landscape-2023

ABOUT THE AUTHOR

Marc Weathers - CEO & Cybersecurity Strategist at Red Rabbit Security

Marc Weathers is the visionary CEO and founder of Red Rabbit Security, a cutting-edge cybersecurity firm dedicated to protecting small and mid-sized businesses from today's most pressing digital threats. With over two decades of experience in information security, Marc has built a reputation as a trusted leader in the fields of threat prevention, compliance, and cyber resilience.

Marc's expertise spans the full cybersecurity spectrum—from penetration testing and risk assessment to advanced threat detection and incident response. Under his leadership, Red Rabbit Security has pioneered a subscription-based cybersecurity model that delivers enterprise-grade protection to businesses that previously lacked access to affordable security solutions. His approach blends technical precision with strategic foresight, empowering clients to stay ahead of ransomware, phishing, business email compromise, and emerging AI-driven attacks.

An advocate for security awareness, Marc frequently conducts cybersecurity training sessions, speaks at industry events, and consults on regulatory compliance for cyber insurance and data privacy laws. His leadership at Red Rabbit Security reflects a core belief: cybersecurity isn't a luxury—it's a business imperative. Marc continues to innovate and inspire in an ever-evolving threat landscape, making Red Rabbit Security a force multiplier for businesses determined to defend what matters most.

Made in the USA
Middletown, DE
01 July 2025